HOW TO GET YOUR MUSIC IN
FILM & TV

RICHARD JAY

P9-DMQ-026

SCHIRMER
TRADE
BOOKS

A Part of **The Music Sales Group**
New York/London/Paris/Sydney/Copenhagen/Berlin/Tokyo/Madrid

Schirmer Trade Books
A Division of Music Sales Corporation, New York

Exclusive Distributors:
Music Sales Corporation
257 Park Avenue South, New York, NY 10010 USA

Music Sales Limited
8/9 Frith Street, London W1D 3JB England

Music Sales Pty. Limited
120 Rothschild Street, Rosebery, Sydney, NSW 2018, Australia

Order No. SCH 10160
International Standard Book Number: 0-8256-7321-6

Printed in the United States of America

Cover Design: Josh Labouve

Library of Congress Cataloging-in-Publication Data
Jay, Richard, 1972-
   How to get your music in film and TV / by Richard Jay.
      p. cm.
   ISBN 0-8256-7321-6 (pbk. : alk. paper)
   1. Music trade--Vocational guidance. 2. Motion pictures and music. 3.
Television and music. I. Title.
   ML3790.J39 2005
   781.5'4'023--dc22
                              2005006020

TABLE OF CONTENTS

Acknowledgements

In writing this book, I would like to thank the following people:
for their help with statistical information: The BPI, the British Library, and the IFPI in London;
for continually being generous with her time: Sindee Levin;
for listening to me talk every week: My students at the European School of Economics;
For being my lifeline for 30 years: My Mum;
Finally,
for putting up with my 25 hours a day, 8 days a week schedule: My wife Maki, without whom none of this would mean anything
— R x

About the Author

Richard Jay was born in 1972 and raised in a typical commuter town outside of London, England. His mother would tell you that even as a child he loved music—this cannot be denied as there are embarrassing photos and home recordings to prove it.

Upon leaving school at the age of sixteen with mediocre exam results, Richard entered the allegedly glamorous world of the music industry by working as a sound engineer at a local recording studio. He quickly grew tired of the engineer life and by his early twenties had immersed himself in the stereo-typical pursuit of starving musicians: The Holy Grail that is "The Record Deal." As is often the case, the longed-for deal didn't actually arrive for a *very* long time—almost ten years—but along the way he had secured a couple of cover recordings of his songs with various major-label artists, and (more importantly) had learned the ups and downs of the music industry.

The business skills he developed in pursuit of those goals led him to create a number of successful companies, chief among them publishing company *Burning Petals Music* and film/TV music tip sheet *CueSheet.net* (the latter sold to Songlink International in 2001).

Richard now lives in the English countryside near Glastonbury, where he is a director of The Music Broker Network, a company that places unsigned artists with film/TV projects, music publishers, and major record companies. In his spare time he lectures at The European School of Economics (London).

He still writes music and his work has been licensed to film and TV production companies worldwide, including Paramount Pictures, Fox, BBC, Columbia Pictures, and many others.

He is no longer looking for a record deal.

Introduction

The global music industry has gone through a tremendous amount of change in the first few years of this new century: Major record companies have merged with each other, well-established independents are downsizing, more artists than usual are having their contracts terminated, and many smaller companies have simply gone out of business. At the time of writing (Spring 2005), the record industry had been through several years of nerve-wracking, rollercoaster statistics.

According to industry body IFPI (International Federation of Phonographic Industries), worldwide sales of music CDs dropped 7.6% in 2003 after a 7% decline in 2002. This is on top of the 5% drop the industry experienced in 2001. In specialist genres, the picture looked even gloomier. For example, according to *Billboard* Dance charts between the summers of 2001 and 2002, when file sharing was starting to reach the mainstream of computer users, this sector shrunk by an incredible 96%.

By mid-2004 the decline had slowed to a further 1.3% drop—but this was hardly cause for celebration. Record sales had seen a slashing of profits almost unprecedented in such a huge industry.

The reasons for this are many and varied, but the availability of so much free music in the form of illegal MP3s was undoubtedly one of the biggest challenges that the creative industries have had to face. With the dual threat and opportunities of the Internet, the record industry has had to work hard to find a new way of selling its "product." Right now the consumer is calling the shots: They want it cheaper than before and they want it now.

While it can't be denied that 2004 was the year that legal online sales started to come of age, the online world is unlikely to quickly become the Holy Grail that many in the record industry had hoped it would. Indeed, according to analysts Jupiter Media, paid downloads only represented about 2% of total music sales in 2004. Even if it were to increase ten-fold in five years, it still represents relatively small numbers to an embattled industry.

It is obvious therefore, that a new way of generating at least part of the substantial income the industry had come to depend on needed to be found. Many executives in the industry believe providing music for use in film and TV is one such area.

The power of music in film cannot be doubted; whether it is Audrey Hepburn's character singing "Moon River" in *Breakfast at Tiffany's,* or the unmistakable opening bars of Monty Normans' "James Bond Theme," music has always had the ability to shortcut to the emotions. More recently, we need only look at blockbusters such as *Titanic* to see how a track featured—however briefly—can promote its associated film. While it's true the creative importance, not to mention relevance to the story, of these particular songs is marginal, it also can't be denied that if the makers of *Titanic* had stayed true to its Irish storyline and asked Celine Dion to sing a traditional Irish folk song, it is unlikely the song would have reached anything like the sales of "My Heart Will Go On" or the 10-million selling soundtrack album featuring that performance.

From a purely financial perspective, placing music in film or TV also makes sense. Over recent years there has been an explosion of TV stations worldwide—whether they be terrestrial, satellite, cable, or even broadband Internet channels. They all need music for one reason or another and they have to pay for it. The film world has not (yet) suffered the kinds of piracy problems the record industry has, so it also represents a huge market for music providers. There is a constant demand for every kind of music imaginable—including many genres for which one would have great difficulty finding a suitable record deal. Solo instrumentalists, such as pianists, violinists, flautists, and guitarists, often do very well from film and TV music because the "space" and intimacy in their music means it can work very well under dialogue. DJs, programmers, rappers, and others involved in electronic or urban music benefit from the fact that producers always want to be seen as being current and appealing to a young, hip audience that gravitates to those genres of music.

Even in more mainstream genres, one only has to look at the career of someone like Vonda Shepard for proof of TV or film's power. Her previously (if you'll forgive me) uneventful career literally exploded from both her and her music being heavily featured in every episode of Fox's long-running *Ally McBeal*. Dido got a helping hand thanks to her performance of the theme to Warner Bros. TV's cult teen show *Roswell*, and The Rembrandts certainly had a career-defining moment thanks to their *Friends* theme song. Even bands like Metallica got in on the act when Buena Vista paid them a record-breaking $1-million (U.S.) advance to write and record a song for *Mission: Impossible 2*. The subsequent soundtrack album reportedly turned a profit of $15-million (U.S.).

Do not think, though, this is an area where the rich multinational music companies are going to have it all their own way. They may have the record distribution scene sown up; they may even have radio stations under their thumb (not to mention on their payroll), but when it comes to getting music into film and TV, the independent music company and artist have a number of "aces" up their sleeves. In many cases, it is true the film and TV companies concerned have relatively small music budgets; but they represent a great opportunity for the smaller indie label, music publisher, or musician to make a deal they're happy with. Major music companies have too much overhead to profit from small deals, but you don't.

To put things in perspective, one use of an unknown, unsigned artist's song on a typical U.S. television network show would (on average) pay the copyright owner(s) a few thousand dollars upfront. Additionally, the writer (and publisher, if there was one) would usually be paid performance royalties every time the show was broadcast (which, if it was sold overseas, could be substantial). If the show was successful and happened to be suitable for release to the public on DVD, perhaps with an accompanying soundtrack CD, additional royalties would be generated from those sales.

That's thousands of dollars going to an artist nobody had ever heard of—and this happens week in, week out.

If you're looking for a record deal right now, I should probably tell you that in order to make a few thousand dollars from record sales you might need to sell as many as 10,000 copies of your album: That's presuming you've paid off the $250,000-plus of your future royalties that your major label has spent on recording and promoting the album.

Oh, and did I mention: If you do what I'm suggesting, not only can you still try and get a record deal with that song, but you've suddenly became a lot more attractive to the record companies and music publishers you've been chasing after?

You see, it is said that most "talent spotters" in the music industry are nothing more than sheep. If you've ever driven your car on a narrow road with a herd of sheep in front of you, you'll get the analogy. Everyone follows everyone else. In the beginning of your career everyone says the same and does the same: Usually, nothing. Often that is the way it stays until you generate some kind of activity yourself, at which point those same people who didn't feel compelled to do anything before are suddenly more interested in you. If you're really lucky and you've managed to, for example, place your song in a big TV show or film, the inelegant scramble from record companies and music publishers can be quite gratifying.

They know that the most difficult and expensive part of selling a record is the marketing. Promotional costs nearly always dwarf those of actually recording the record in the first place, so any way the artist can take a shortcut to capture the record-buying public's attention has got to be a good thing for all concerned.

Read on…

ONE

WHY USE MUSIC?

*T*here are many reasons why a music copyright holder would want to license their music into films and TV shows; but why do these projects need music in the first place?

The first use of music with film—not that long ago, in fact—occurred with the advent of silent films. Pianists, in a theater, sitting to one side of a cinema screen, accompanied the on-screen action. By all accounts, the musicians in question never used to play the same thing twice, so it is debatable how much their offerings added to the picture. Nonetheless, this is how the film score began.

Soon, the composers of the day realized some order was needed so they set about writing books of suitable piano music. Not content with writing for one musician, soon small orchestra's were being employed to add drama and emotion to films. Even film star Charlie Chaplin—who incidentally was an underrated composer as well—penned music for some of his own films.

Needless to say, there wasn't much capability for playing in precise timing with the actors' movements, so it must have come as somewhat of a welcome relief when composers were able to write, record, and synchronize their score with the new "talking" pictures. Still, while there were highly commendable scores from the likes of Max Steiner and Alfred Newman, in general the musical offerings were not playing anything more than a background role, deliberately not drawing attention to themselves.

This all changed though in 1935 when Austrian composer Erich Korngold wrote the dramatic score for the Errol Flynn movie,

1

Captain Blood. This symphonic work heralded the dawn of the film score as an important weapon in the director's arsenal.

Before too long, the idea of using pre-existing music, alongside that written especially for the project, became popular. One of the most notable was Max Steiner's score to *Casablanca,* which also included the French and German national anthems and, of course, Herman Hupfeld's famous theme, "As Time Goes By." The great pop and musical theater composers of the time, such as George and Ira Gershwin, Johnny Mercer, and Cole Porter were also now writing both songs and incidental music for film.

Naturally, when television arrived in the 1950s, it too used music as an integral part of visual entertainment. Its usage of music to this day has, if anything, increased and there is a much wider variety of genres heard now than in those early days.

Let's be clear on what is meant by "music in film and TV." I'm not referring to music entertainment shows that play music videos or have artists performing their latest track. I am referring to situations in which a third party chooses to use someone else's music in their production, as an accompaniment to whatever is happening on screen. For example:

- A love story features a couple having a romantic dinner in a restaurant. It might include background music scored by a composer or a pianist playing on-screen behind the actors.
- A violent story set in a ghetto: A "gangsta" rap track plays prominently during a drive-by shooting and subsequent police chase.

These are just two examples and each one requires payment to the respective music copyright holder(s). In the first example, music was used in the background to make the scene seem natural. Many restaurants have music playing quietly in the background and in a romantic scene the viewer expects romantic music. So unless the director was deliberately going for an unnatural feel, he would have had virtually no choice but to use music.

The second example, a featured performance, is a different kind of usage. In this instance, the use of an urban artist would likely lend considerable credibility and authenticity to the picture. The acting may be bad—perhaps matched only by the predictability of the script—but with the right choice of music, particularly if it's from a known artist with a certain image, this film could play well to its target audience.

Many people are not even aware of music being used in the background, but if you've ever seen a dramatic scene from a film that doesn't have any music at all, you'll quickly become aware something is missing. Because of the skill required to make this work, there aren't many well-known examples, but (depending on your definition of music) good ones include *The Blair Witch Project* (1999), *Forbidden Planet* (1956), and Alfred Hitchcock's *The Birds;* the famous car chase in *Bullitt* (1968) is also without music. Complete silence can certainly be used to dramatic effect too. But for all our sakes, let's hope it's not too often!

Rest assured that any intelligent person in the film and TV world doesn't need to be told the importance of music to a project: This is one sales pitch you don't have to make.

The 1980s was the decade in which Hollywood realized the promotional potential of having a predominantly song-based score. This was no doubt prompted by the runaway success of 1977's *Saturday Night Fever.* Up until this point, most film soundtracks consisted of a strong opening theme and background incidental music—both usually instrumental. A director could rely on big names, such as John Williams, to create equally big scores to reinforce whatever mood or emotion they were trying to achieve. Occasionally a film would have a song in it, but it invariably felt "tacked on." Often, it was not written by the composer of the film and therefore thematically did not flow with the rest of the music.

It was obviously noted though, that the few songs present in major films seemed to chart on an impressively consistent basis. Indeed, some evergreen songs were born through their inclusion in a film, one example is Burt Bacharach and Hal David's, "Raindrops Keep Fallin' On My Head."

Add to this the fact that multinationals of the day, such as PolyGram or Sony either had, or developed, film companies alongside their music divisions, and the less-than-unpredictable result was a proliferation of films featuring copyrights from their associated music division. Though I can't claim to have inside knowledge of typical financial arrangements in these situations, it is clear that a multinational would rather have its film division pay its music division rather than pay an outside music company.

It is also obvious to me that if a multinational is giving a large amount of money to its film division, they would much rather cross-promote an artist from another division than an artist from an entirely unrelated company. The company could push this decision, almost regardless of whether the film's creative team felt the related artist's music was the best choice.

Undoubtedly some of the worst examples of the latter were the tediously banal American teen-oriented films of the 1980s, which seemed to incorporate little in the way of artistic control (and not just in their choice of music). A quick glance at the publishing and/or record company credits for such films will invariably reveal one big, happy, corporate family.

In conclusion then, though creative purists like myself may balk, the idea makes perfect sense:

- The film was more profitable, by reducing its dependence on external music providers.
- The artists included in the film had their profiles raised considerably, often resulting in greater record sales and profits for the sister company.
- Greater sales and promotion of the record resulted in cross-promotion of the film and increased ticket sales.
- The soundtrack CD album could be expected to sell in far greater numbers than if it consisted of instrumental score music.

For the multinational, it's a win-win situation. Of course the independent film or TV producer has to settle for a little less, as they invariably won't profit from the career of an artist whose song is included in their project. Regardless, they still enjoy the considerable benefits of cross-promotion and maybe royalty participation in the soundtrack album, as well.

TWO

WHERE DOES THE MUSIC COME FROM?

*B*efore you learn how to get your music into film and TV, you need to be completely clear on the basic principles of the music business. While nobody will expect you to be an expert on industry law or practice, if you are completely clueless, you run the risk of looking like an amateur: Something to be avoided in any business transaction. In a worst-case scenario, an obviously "green" musician could be taken advantage of by an unscrupulous person, so take some time to acquaint yourself with the facts.

Music Publishers

A music publisher owns and/or controls music—including lyrics, if there are any—and earns its money by granting permission for its use to third parties.

Publishers and the people they work with only make money if a third party wants to use their music. A typical use would be a record company's artist wanting to record a version of a song owned by a music publisher.

A lot of unsigned musicians, particularly songwriters, put all of their energy into finding a publisher and getting their work published. They seem to think that once they achieve this, their career is made and money will inevitably follow. This is wholly incorrect. Merely signing a contract with a music publisher does not generate any money. At best, it simply means that somebody else has a financial incentive to ensure that your music is being used by others and will therefore do their job properly; but even that shouldn't be assumed.

These days, the term "music publisher" is something of a misnomer. Publishing music, in the old-fashion sense of printing sheet music, is now a very small revenue stream for modern publishers. That was not the case one-hundred years ago. Before gramophones, radio, TV, and the myriad entertainment options we have today, buying printed music to perform on your piano at home was a popular activity among the general public. Even fifty years ago it was common for every member of a family to have a song they would be required to perform for their relatives at special occasions. In many ways, this communal performance by amateur musicians and singers was the forerunner to the craze of karaoke. Today, however, publishers choose to license print rights to companies that specialize in printing sheet music and songbooks

Music publishers work with lyricists, composers, and song-writers. They only work with artists or performers directly if they also happen to be writers. Each of these people assigns the copyright in their work to the publisher so the publisher becomes the copyright holder. This could be on a permanent basis (i.e., life of copyright). However, a temporary assignment is more common, depending upon the individual's negotiating power when they enter into a contract.

Well-known publishers include EMI Music, Sony-ATV, Warner/Chappell, BMG Music, and Universal Music. But there are also thousands of lesser-known publishers around the world.

Record Companies

A record company owns and controls recordings and typically earns its money by selling copies of those recordings to the general public—either through retail outlets or by granting the right to other record companies to do so. Although they control the material recording, they do not control the underlying music and lyrics, which are always controlled by music publishers.

Record companies work with artists and numerous other support people such as record producers, musicians, and video producers. Each of these people invariably licenses or assigns the ownership rights in their work to the record company so that the record company becomes the copyright holder. This could be on a permanent or temporary basis, depending upon their contract.

Mechanical License

A mechanical license is formal permission from a music publisher for a third party to reproduce a specific copyright owned by the publisher, in "mechanical" form. Again, this is a rather old-fashion sounding expression, but it refers to any kind of machine that plays back music. Examples include CD, DVD, video, music boxes, and toys.

The most common form of mechanical license would be for a record company whose artist wishes to record a song for commercial release. For each copy of the record sold, a royalty is payable by the record company to the publisher, who takes his commission and then pays the writers.

In the U.S., the rate is set on an annual basis by the Copyright Royalty Tribunal with reference to the Consumer Price Index (CPI): In 2004/2005, the rate is 8.5¢ for up to five minutes (or $1.65 per minute, if greater than five minutes). In 2006, the rate is 9.1¢ or $1.75. In most other countries, the rate is defined as a percentage of the products dealer price—currently 8.5% in the U.K. and 9.5% in continental Europe—divided by the number of songs on the product. Consequently a ten-song album would pay 0.85% or 0.95% respectively, per song. This is known as a mechanical royalty.

Many music publishers use a licensing organization to collect their royalties for them, to ease their own administration workload. Examples include the Harry Fox Agency and AMRA (American Mechanical Rights Agency, Inc.) in the United States, MCPS (Mechanical Copyright Protection Society) in the U.K., and GEMA in Germany. These organizations take a small commission for their services but without them a music publisher would have to deal individually with each company who wanted to use their copyrights.

Synchronization License

A synchronization ("sync") license is formal permission from a music publisher for a third party to reproduce a specific copyright owned by them, in synchronization with moving pictures.

The rates charged for the sync license are purely a matter of negotiation between the publisher ("Licensor") and user ("Licensee").

Performing Right License

A performing right license is formal permission from a music publisher for a third party to perform in public any copyright owned by them. This includes fee-paying audiences, such as concerts or films, as well as non fee-paying audiences such as hotels or even elevators. Any performance of copyrighted music, whether a recording or live performance, that takes place outside of the home, is regarded as a public performance and will usually require a license.

Individual writers also have performing rights that they can grant, as provided to them by their country's copyright laws. Both writers and publishers nearly always assign these rights to a performing-rights organization who administer them on their behalf. In the U.S., there are three organizations (ASCAP, BMI, and SESAC), though a writer can only be a member of one at a time. Consequently, there is an element of competition between them to attract writers. Most other countries only have one organization, such as the PRS in the U.K or APRA in Australia.

These organizations, wherever possible, monitor music played on radio/TV, performed at venues, etc. They then distribute performance royalties to the writer and publisher of the music. Where this is impractical—such as a hotel lobby—a yearly flat fee is charged, and royalties are distributed to the writers and publishers of the most popular music on a pro-rata basis.

Societies in most countries around the world fulfill the same task and distribute the money to the relevant PRO's (performing-rights organizations) in other countries. So, for example, if you are a U.S. writer affiliated with ASCAP and you have a piece of music performed in Japan, JASRAC will collect the income due and pay ASCAP on your behalf. They, in turn, should pay you.

Master Use License

A master use license is formal permission from a record company for a third party to reproduce a specific recording owned by them, in timed synchronization with moving pictures.

The rates charged for the license are purely a matter of negotiation between the record company ("Licensor") and user ("Licensee"). The licensee will also require a synchronization license from the record company.

COPYRIGHT 101

In the beginning…the time was March 1847 and the place was Paris, France…two friends were enjoying a meal at a café. One was the French songwriter, Ernest Bourget. By coincidence, his music was performed during their visit. So, when he was presented the bill for the meal, he refused to pay for it on the grounds that the café had been "consuming" his music while he was consuming their food. As he had not been paid for the performance of his music, he therefore felt it was unfair for him to be expected to pay for the food served. He subsequently sued the café, and the court—in a landmark decision—found in his favor.

Shortly thereafter, a French society was formed to protect the interests of creators' rights and collect performance royalties on their behalf.

Copyright is a kind of "property" which arises automatically upon the creation of a work.

Music, photographs, and books are just three examples of work protected by international copyright laws. Song titles and ideas cannot be copyrighted. Copyright is identified by the © symbol, though the right of ownership is actually created automatically as soon as something is created and recorded in permanent form (written, recorded, etc.). However, to get full protection under the law, it's always a good idea to register your work with the U.S. Copyright Office.

Protection generally lasts for up to 70 years after the death of the creator—though exact terms differ from country to country and depend on when the work was created. If there is more than one creator, then the period of protection commences after the death of the last living creator.

In the U.S., copyright is controlled by the Copyright Act of 1976, which replaced the 1909 act. In the U.K., copyright is controlled by the Copyright, Designs & Patents act of 1988, which replaced the 1956 act.

Each country has its own copyright societies and law; but less-developed countries are many decades behind the most advanced countries and do not have collection societies or, sometimes, even adequate copyright laws.

If someone utilizes copyrighted music without first seeking the permission of the copyright holder, then they are infringing copyright and are liable for prosecution. Anyone else who is a party to infringement can also be prosecuted. This is why whenever you sign any kind of legal agreement with someone who wishes to use your music, they will always require a statement that says your music is entirely original and does not infringe upon anybody else's copyright. So, for example, if you signed a publishing deal for a piece of music which you said you wrote but was actually based on someone else's work, it would be the publisher who would be accused of copyright infringement. If they were taken to court by their accuser, they would no doubt sue you for breach of contract.

Piracy is a specific form of infringement, where someone reproduces recordings owned by a third party and makes them available to the public without seeking the permission of the owners. It is irrelevant whether such an act is done for commercial gain or not. Many die-hard fans will make available live recordings of performances by their favorite bands and sell them at record fairs or via the Internet, simply because the record company decided not to do so. Invariably, it is not the intention of the fan to purely earn money for themselves, but rather to share their passion for the music. Well intentioned though it maybe, this is still theft.

THREE

Opportunities

Marketing your wares to every relevant person you can think of is a major part of generating opportunities for yourself and we shall be looking at the necessary skills in the next chapter. But there are a number of more direct, less speculative ways in which you can find out precisely who is looking for music or likely to need it in the near future.

Project Types
There are many different kinds of film and TV projects that need music. Here is a rundown of the most common projects:

Student Films
Budget range: None to very low

Most successful composers serve their apprenticeship by doing a few student films. It really should be left at just "a few," unless there are special reasons for doing more. Given the financial constraints, I can think of no good reason why anyone would want to license material to a student film. It is unlikely to reach a wide audience and therefore does not have any promotional benefit.

Low-Budget Films
Budget range: Very low to low

Whether to get involved in a low-budget feature is always a tough call. There are always going to be films such as *The Blair Witch Project* that break through from nowhere. If this film had called for music, then, at the time, there wouldn't have been much competition to get involved, which could have turned out to be a great career move for the chosen musician(s). On the other hand, most low-budget films end up in small "art house" cinemas or doing the festival circuit: If indeed, they do anything. This one calls for discretion. It could be a good opportunity to make relationships with up-and-coming industry folk or it could be a gigantic waste of time. Choose wisely.

TV Documentaries
Budget range: Usually low, occasionally medium

Writing original music for documentaries (for it is usually commissioned, rarely licensed) is not exactly a 'get-rich-quick' scheme. However there are a number of attractive benefits. From a creative point of view, the composer may be given the opportunity to write a genre of music that is rarely called for in fiction-based programming. In the past week alone I have seen documentaries set in the Andes Mountains and Egypt. In both cases, composers were hired to write contemporary interpretations of a region's traditional music.

Additionally, the subject matter of many documentaries is timeless and not specific to the country of origin, thereby increasing the odds of repeat showings around the world—each time generating performance royalties for the composer. For example, if the Discovery Channel made a documentary about the Brazilian rainforests, it is likely to be shown unchanged in many countries of the world (except for the narration being in the local language). Although typically produced by small, independent production companies, an increasing number are relatively expensive productions involving two or more broadcasters from different countries. The BBC is also well known for documentaries and works closely with a number of overseas networks, such as those from Canada, Australia, Japan, and elsewhere. Obviously having worked for such prestigious networks as the BBC (U.K.), NHK (Japan), or Discovery (U.S.) does a lot of good for the composer's résumé.

TV Soap Operas/Sitcoms

Budget range: Low to medium

Music in "soaps" and sitcoms tends to be approached differently according to the part of the world in which it is being made. North American and South East Asian/Japanese TV tends to be wall-to-wall music, sound effects, and dialogue, whereas British programming is invariably a lot more subtle. Western European and Australian TV is usually somewhere between the two. Consequently, while all will usually require opening and closing music, it is rare to find, for example, a U.K. sitcom that features songs playing in the foreground—or rarer still, a U.K. soap opera with incidental music. Bear these precedents in mind when studying your local market. North American, Australian, and U.K. shows often air in many different countries, so performance royalties can be sizeable.

TV Movie/Mini-Series

Budget range: Medium to occasionally high

Usually made by film studios or TV broadcasters, the subject matter of TV movies and mini-series varies enormously and therefore so do their musical requirements. Broadly speaking, a period drama is likely to require a composer to provide original music, whereas a more contemporary setting may rely on licensing pre-existing songs. Budgets aren't a problem, but obviously there is a lot of competition. Repeats are not as common as with other TV shows, so the performance income is not as lucrative.

Feature Films

Budget range: Medium to very high

Obviously this is the main aspiration of most people when they think of music in film. It is usually the highest paid, the most prestigious, and offers the greatest likelihood of career benefits (such as soundtrack sales). Indeed the only negative thing to be aware of is the fact that, unlike virtually everywhere else, cinemas in the U.S. don't pay performance royalties. Elsewhere cinema owners are required to pay a royalty (sometimes known as theatrical royalties) to the local performing-rights organization: They in turn pay the composer, songwriter, and publisher.

Finding Opportunities

Websites and tip sheets are excellent sources to mine for possible opportunities. In late 2001 I founded a company called *CueSheet.net* which produced a twice-monthly listing of TV and film projects specifically looking for music. This would include opportunities for composers to create new scores, as well as songwriters, publishers, or record companies to place pre-existing tracks. This was by no means a new concept—I can't claim to have invented the "tip sheet"—but it very quickly attracted a subscriber base consisting of many major and independent music companies.

Every two weeks, either an associate or I would phone up as many music supervisors as we could to find out about their current projects and music needs. If they were feeling generous or having an especially difficult time finding what they were looking for, they would tell us about their projects. In most cases we would find out the name of the project and which company was producing it, the leading actors, a brief synopsis of the story, and—crucially—their ideas on what kind of music they were looking for. Obviously, the last bit of information was the most important, but it is often useful to know the story behind the project as well. If you're pitching songs, then maybe there is a track in your catalog with a similar lyric, or if you're a composer, maybe you have some music using instruments from the country or period in which the story is set. If nothing else, it's a great education as to who the big players are in the world of music supervision. I sold it exactly a year later, so I have no vested interest now, but I do recommend you take a look at its Website as it is still offers essentially the same services.

A similar bulletin is published by New York-based New on the Charts *(www.notc.com)*. They have a monthly publication detailing various opportunities for music copyright holders and their Soundtrack Newsletter is part of it. Compared to *CueSheet.net,* it is smaller in size and tends to deal mainly with independent filmmakers, but it is nonetheless a valuable and cost-effective service.

For those who are happy to do a little more research, there are various other resources that, though not specifically aimed at the music world, are nonetheless equally valuable. The most up-to-date list can be found at *www.Training4Music.biz/resources,* but here are some of the most important ones I have found in my travels:

www.mandy.com: At the time of writing, it certainly won't win any awards for outstanding Web design, but there's no denying Mandy's is a great place to find low-budget indie feature or short films in need of music. Not a week goes by without at least one such request from a U.S. or U.K. producer. It is fair to say though, we are definitely talking low budget here…if not *no*-budget, so an extra-thorough investigation of any project you may be thinking of getting involved in is definitely recommended. Still, the price of accessing Mandy's (i.e. free) just can't be beat.

www.inhollywood.com: This is an online database of North American film and TV projects in development or production. It provides contact information along with cast and synopsis info. You can 'tag' various projects you are interested in and receive updates as the project progresses.

www.hollywoodreporter.com: *The Hollywood Reporter,* along with *Variety,* is the main source of news and gossip in the American production industry. In their Tuesday editions, they list many film projects at various stages of production. Ordinarily, they would not disclose the name of any music supervisor and other details are brief, at best. Still, it provides you with good information as to which companies are producing which projects. An alternative to purchasing their print edition is the Internet access that allows you to view these production files on a pay-per-view basis.

www.productionweekly.com: A much more advanced version of the above is *Production Weekly,* which is delivered by fax or e-mail every week. It lists many U.S. films in production (and some in Canada and the U.K.), along with synopsis and cast/crew list. It also tells you at what stage their production is in, so you don't waste time contacting people who are a couple of years away from postproduction.

www.crimsonuk.com: As you can probably guess from the Web address, *Crimson* is a British company, but they have various publications detailing British, European, and North American productions that are looking for various services including music.

www.pcrnewsletter.com: When trying to find out about projects which will be requiring music, it is worth thinking about what else these projects may need and how they may go about finding those services. One obvious need that springs to mind (at least for fictional projects) is actors. The U.K.'s *PCR Newsletter* is a listing of both film and TV projects in pre-production looking for actors (and their representatives). It's also an under-used information source for the music industry. If a project is looking for actors, sooner or later, they are likely to need music.

www.hcdonline.com: HCD is a well-established publisher of contact directories that are now available on line via a monthly subscription. Their premiere publication, the *Hollywood Creative Directory,* has thousands of suitable contacts.

www.filmmusic.net: The main organization for film and TV composers, which provides—among other things—a "Jobwire" supplying information on (predominantly) TV and low-budget features looking for composers and/or songs to license.

www.filefx.co.uk: A series of print directories updated every few months. They are particularly good for researching European advertising agencies and U.K. film/TV production companies, as they list every significant member of the staff.

The Blue Book of British Broadcasting: An annual directory listing the various departments of British regional and national TV broadcasters (such as the BBC and ITV).

With some effort, you'll find leads in a variety of places. Now it's time to chase those leads and try to get your music placed in a project.

FOUR

NETWORKING

Knowing what opportunities are out there is half the battle. But as important as this information is, it will come to nothing if you don't present yourself and your work to the right people.

Who's in Charge of What in Film and TV
In the film and TV industry, there are a number of key people you need to get to know. First, is the film director. Often likened to a record producer, the director is the person who is ultimately in control of the creative aspects of the project. As such, directors can often be useful allies if they strongly believe in an artist or composer. For TV projects, the producer, executive producer, or line producer usually handles this creative role. At the larger TV networks or film studios, there will be a vice president of music or music supervisor who (naturally) gets very involved in music choices.

In film projects, the producer arguably plays a less creative role, as they oversee the entire project and are often "second in command" to the director. However, they often have an equal say in who is hired (or who is not), and they are ultimately responsible for the approval of all financial matters. Nonetheless, it should be realized that the importance of the producer is relevant to whether the project is destined for film or TV, and whether the production company is large enough to have its own music division.

The editor has a much wider responsibility than just the synchronization and editing of music to picture; but he is usually in charge of this as well unless there is a dedicated music editor. Either

17

way, the usefulness of building relationships with an editor, particularly a music editor, should not be underestimated.

Editors are responsible for the creation of the temporary music soundtrack, used in the early stages of editing, in lieu of a finished score or licensed music.

Commonly referred to as the "temp track," the music used often comes from a variety of sources. Certainly the individual's own music collection may be used extensively, but many times the more astute editor will use music which could feasibly end up in the finished project, such as easily licensable masters from unsigned artists or tracks from a new composer's show reel. This avoids the rather common problem of the director or producer falling in love with music from the temp track when it would be prohibitively expensive—or even impossible—to license. Composers hoping to be hired by a certain director or producer might like to suggest that he use their work in the temp track free of charge, precisely so that he may fall in love with it.

Finally, we come to the role of music supervisor, who is the most obvious bridge between the music and film/TV worlds. The music supervisor may be a freelance individual, part of a team of independent supervisors, or employed full time directly by a film or TV company.

Historically, music supervisors were charged with gaining permission from the owners of the music copyright to use their work in a film or TV show. These days however, it is common for them to be far more involved in the creative aspects of the soundtrack. This may include putting forward suggestions for score composers or finding suitable tracks to license. Occasionally, these creative abilities come at the expense of a less-detailed knowledge of copyright and legal considerations than would previously have been expected from a music supervisor. This has given birth to the job of the so-called music consultants and clearance companies who are only concerned with the actual paperwork involved in licensing, leaving the supervisor to concentrate on the music itself.

There are two kinds of music supervisors: The independent and those employed by a major film studio or TV network. The latter has a large team of people around them to whom they can delegate certain parts of their job, and with whom they have (hopefully) built a strong working relationship. In the often fast-paced world of licensing and commissioning, this can ease the workload for all concerned. However, as we discussed earlier, many of these major companies have associated music divisions to whom they will look first for their music needs—thereby reducing opportunities for the "outside" music provider.

The independent music supervisor on the other hand, does not have such formal, potentially restrictive alliances and can therefore choose from a wider range of sources right off the bat. In some cases, they may also have a small team of personnel around them assisting with legal and financial administration.

Helping Hands in the Music Industry

It can be tough for a musician to make contact with these key people on their own. Luckily, there are many people in the recording industry whose job involves—and even depends on—promoting your music.

From the music world, we have the agent, music publisher, record company, and broker. All of these people have one interest in common: The desire to place music they (or their associates) own or control in as many film and TV projects as they possibly can.

The agent typically represents a number of composers who specialize in writing new, original music for film and TV. Typically, the composer pays a commission on each job to their agent, who has usually found the job or at the very least taken care of negotiating the best deal possible. The commission payable would rarely exceed 20% of the total fee. The agent should also make efforts to license the back catalog of the composer.

Most major music publishers and record companies, plus an increasing number of independents, have dedicated film and TV personnel whose sole job is to find suitable projects into which they can license their music. You'll remember from our introduction, music companies who were previously happy to concentrate on record sales have to find new avenues of income generation. So, it should come as no surprise to you that many companies now have specialist roles like this.

For those companies that cannot afford to hire or dedicate someone to this role, there is the broker or licensing agent. These are people who do the same job as the in-house film and TV department, but for a number of different companies. I work as a broker and represent a number of different labels, publishers, and unsigned artists from all parts of the world, working in most genres of music. The advantage of a broker is that the client benefits from the services of a dedicated film and TV expert, but at a much-reduced cost; the disadvantage is the broker's often paid on a commission basis. But as the saying goes, "It is better to have 50% of something, than 100% of nothing."

Networking for the Composer/Musician

How do you even get to speak to these people though? There is a fundamental difference between how a composer should market themselves and how an artist or songwriter with pre-existing material should market themselves.

Let's first take a look at the path the composer/musician would take.

A composer is hired to realize the musical vision of the film/TV project. The composer needs to be aware they are being paid to do a job and if they disagree with the directions given, beyond a certain level of constructive debate, they must concede and undertake the work that is required of them.

On one level, this may seem like an unappealing scenario and goes against the very self-expression which leads to creating music in the first place. However, the spirit of teamwork, not to mention the potentially perfect marriage of music with pictures, brings its own high rewards.

The teamwork the composer-director/producer relationship demands requires great personal skills, so the composer should make it a priority to start networking.

For the beginning composer with few credits to speak of, it is safest to assume they need to "work their way up the ladder" in the time honored tradition. Therefore, they should go where the beginning directors and producers go.

In the United States, this would include organizations such as Association of Independent Feature Film Producers (AIFFP), in the

U.K. this would include PACT or NPA, and in Australia it would be The Australian Screen Directors Association. You can find links to these, and similar organizations, at *www.Training4Music.biz/resources*.

Despite the huge advances in telecommunications over the past decade, the composer will unfortunately still be disadvantaged if he does not live in a center of film and TV production. In the U.S., this would be New York and Los Angeles, in Canada it would be Vancouver. Outside of North America, certainly London is the principal source of English-speaking film production but, in common with Australia, so few films are produced it does not represent a major avenue for music creators.

It is not impossible to get good-quality work outside these regions but the vast majority of postproduction tends to be done there, making it an ideal base for the composer (who does much of his work during postproduction).

Therefore, to avoid potentially losing work by being known as living out of town, there are a number of services that can hide your geographic location—such as voice and fax messages which can be received on a normal telephone number but transferred via the Internet or a non-geographical number. You could also rent a P.O. box or use a mail-forwarding service. I'm not suggesting you actually lie about your place of residence, of course, but it would be a shame to lose the chance of a job simply because you had an undesirable address. Once someone has heard your work and is impressed enough to contact you, then that would be a good time to tell them your precise location.

Agents

It is an early goal of many new composers to obtain an agent at the first opportunity. Principally, this is because the composer believes the agent knows "everyone" in the film and TV world that is worth knowing and work will, therefore, be much easier to get.

The truth of the matter is, while a good agent is definitely someone worth having on your side, a good agent will be unlikely to work with you until you have a good résumé and are already generating regular business for yourself anyway. Agents are business people who earn their living by taking a commission from the fees they earn for their clients. It is not their job to take a composer with little in the way of credible or "top-drawer" work and elevate them to the echelons of Hollywood.

There are many, many more composers looking for agents than there are agents looking for composers.

That said, agents would not exist if it weren't for composers and the music they create, so obviously there may come a time when appointing an agent is a real possibility. Consider it a long-term pitch and market to them in the same manner as anyone else in this book.

Networking for the Songwriter

The artist/writer is at a distinct advantage in the marketing of themselves, for a number of reasons.

First and foremost, as they are usually promoting pre-existing work, it rarely makes any difference what part of the world they live in. Unlike the collaborative relationship between a composer and director, there is no collaborative work involved in placing a track in a film: Consequently, if your material is good enough, it makes no difference if you live in South Africa or Southern California.

Additionally, the song itself (invariably) was created to please its maker rather than anyone else. In other words, whereas the composer has to check his ego at the door and provide a service to the filmmaker, the artist or songwriter has the undoubted luxury of only having to please themselves.

Finally, there is this undisputable fact: Original songs generate higher fees than commissioned music (not only at the licensing stage but also from the American PROs). Arguments for and against this practice could fill an entire book, so I won't try to present them here. Just be aware of it.

Music Publishers

In many ways, the music publisher fulfills the same function for the songwriter as the agent does for the composer (though there are some vitally important differences with regard to copyright and income that are discussed later in the book). Like the agent, a publisher does not earn any money unless its client (or his work) is being used and paid for; though it must be said the usage need not have necessarily been generated by the agent/publisher for them to financially benefit from it. In other words, a composer or artist/songwriter who is actively pursuing all opportunities that come their way, would still have to pay a commission to their agent and/or publisher even if the commission or license had come entirely through his own efforts rather than that of his representative.

Invariably, the legal relationship with an agent will be of shorter duration than that with a publisher. I stress *legal* relationship, simply because even if you are no longer talking to or working with a publisher to whom you previously signed your work, they could potentially still own the copyright to it. Most publishing deals call for the copyright to be assigned to the publisher, potentially for the life of copyright. Whereas the relationship with an agent does not usually entail any transfer of copyright, so it would only tie you down for a few years at a time.

A composer can, and often does, have a music publisher

A songwriter can have an agent (or manager)

An artist often has an agent and/or manager but will only have a music publisher if they wrote (or co-wrote) the song

However, if your goal is licensing music into film and TV, the composer/agent and songwriter/publisher is likely to be the most beneficial relationship.

Networking for All
Regardless of whether you're a composer, artist, or whatever, meeting with music supervisors will always be high on your list of priorities. The Film Music Network, based in Los Angeles, but with a chapter in New York too, has events attended by music supervisors throughout the year. Many of them are educational in nature so you can learn while networking. You can find more information at *www.filmmusic.net*.

The long-running music and film conference South by

Southwest (SXSW), held every Spring in Austin, Texas could be useful too. It's very much music *and* film, rather than music with film: Two separate festivals held at the same time, but obviously there's a lot of cross-pollination between the two camps if you stay for the whole event. You can find more information at *www.sxsw.com*.

The Billboard/Hollywood Reporter Film & TV Music Conference is aimed at a slightly different audience. Held in L.A., usually in early winter, this event is not cheap to attend, but if your networking skills are up to it, you'll never get so many music supervisors and executives in one room at the same time again. More information is available at *www.billboardevents.com*.

Of course, even if you don't get many opportunities to meet with music supervisors, you should still get to know who's who. Fortunately for us, the best way of doing that is by watching a lot of film and TV—or at least that was how I justified our new 200-channel satellite TV to my wife!

There is no better way to get to know who the most successful music supervisors are, and maybe even determine their musical preferences, than watching the latest hit shows and blockbusters. You'll need to be quick though when watching the credits—or have a video recorder standing by—to catch the name of the person responsible. You should always be sure to educate yourself on the most powerful people as you never know when you might come across them.

FIVE

MARKETING YOURSELF

Once you have established who the target audience is, the job of marketing begins. If there is one thing I have learned over the past fifteen years that I've been doing this it is that marketing is *everything*. A poorly written, poorly performed, and poorly produced record can still achieve phenomenal sales if it is well marketed. If you think that is an exaggeration—and I perfectly understand why you'd think that—consider this:

In the U.K. during the mid-1990s, there was a particular #1 record that was so unbelievably awful rumors began to circulate that it was the result of a bet between two major label presidents as to who could make the worst record. The song—"No Way, No Way" by the girl-group Vanilla—was dire, the video amateurish, and the "talent" non-existent. The very fact that this song went to #1 demonstrates either that the British public love irony even more than everyone thought, or—more likely—we all have very different ideas of what is good music and what is bad.

The mistake many people make when trying to find their way through the music business, is to concentrate on the former (music) to the detriment of the latter (business). Knowing, as you do now, that I believe marketing to be the most important thing in your career, you may think that I would advise against you spending time becoming the best musician or writer you can be: But you'd be wrong. When your music has been marketed to perfection and everyone knows one of your melodies, you and I both will be glad that you do have talent and you worked hard to make the best tracks you could. In the meantime though, just don't ever forget this is an industry, like any other, that exists to make money.

While there are plenty of people within the industry that love music and its creators, that doesn't give anyone an excuse to ignore basic rules of marketing, business, manners, or anything else. Those people who ignore the "rules," yet still succeed do so by luck alone.

While purists may disagree, when marketing music—at least on a business-to-business level—you would be well advised to imagine your music as a "product," rather than as a piece of art. It may surprise you to learn in the record industry, music is routinely referred to in just this way.

So, if we take the view that composition abilities or pre-existing songs are products, what is the best way to market them?

In any form of marketing, there are a number of key points that need to be considered. Principally:

1. What does the potential customer want?
2. What price are they willing to pay?
3. If they haven't worked with you before, how can they be convinced to take a risk and trust you? (In the case of composers, where the "customer" cannot hear the finished product until many weeks after he has commissioned it, this is even more important.)
4. All things being equal, why would they choose you or your work?

Compounding these four basic points are further issues, such as does the customer actually know what they want? There can be few composers who, at one time or another, have not faced the most frustrating of scenarios where a customer pressures him into providing something the composer advised against—only to have the customer turn around and agree the composer was right to advise against the idea in the first place.

Price is inextricably linked with "value." Metallica's reported advance of $1-million on record sales to write an original song for *Mission: Impossible 2* was undoubtedly a high price, but in terms of value to Buena Vista (the customer), the reported $15-million profit from the soundtrack album means that ultimately the price was justified—even cheap by comparison—if you deem Metallica's song to be important to the sales of the album.

As mentioned already in the introduction, people in the creative industries are notoriously uneasy about taking risks. Often, the reason an unknown composer is hired is because the rate the customer is willing to pay is so low as to give them no choice but to work with someone new. Of course, that's not an ideal way to get a job, but you could probably turn it into a positive situation in the long run. A better situation though, would be to get the job by addressing their concerns about working with someone with whom they have no history.

Finally, even if they have worked with you before or are not concerned by the fact they haven't, they still need specific reasons why they should choose you for this specific project. They will need to hear your unique selling point.

Unique Selling Point (USP)

A USP is a fact about you and your music that sets you apart from everyone else your contact is talking to. It should also be an attribute that no one else shares, though I concede uniqueness is a pretty rare thing.

Of course, many people might argue all music by its very nature is unique anyway. I'd probably agree with that, but bear in mind you may be selling to someone who would not normally choose to listen to your genre of music so they may need a little help in coming to a decision. We all hear music that doesn't appeal to us and in many cases we think it all sounds the same: If you had to license a piece of music from a genre you had no interest in, you'd probably have some difficulty telling good from bad, so if one of the artists/composers had an identifiable USP, then you'd be more likely to deal with them. So, you need to establish your USP(s). Everyone has them.

For example, you may have a particular production style or a singer who has a very jazzy voice but actually performs dance music. I play a hammered dulcimer. If I was pitching to a project that required world music, that would definitely be a USP, but I also wrote some of my favorite pop songs on it (which of course was a USP when I was pitching them as virtually nobody would write a pop song on a hammered dulcimer!).

USPs can also come from your résumé. If you've worked with, or have been supported by someone well known in the industry, then you should definitely mention it.

Unless you have an extremely impressive USP ("I had a Platinum-selling single last year in America") you need to develop as many of them as you can because not all USPs will be appropriate for every project.

Advertising and Publicity

One way to add to that list of USPs and to make a decision-maker more apt to take a risk on you is to demonstrate that other people in the industry are aware of you and your work. Advertising and publicity are two very different ways to get your name out there.

Q: What is the difference between advertising and publicity?
A: Publicity is free; advertising is not.

Advertising is one fairly easy way to get your name into a magazine or trade publication, but unless you have money to burn, don't do it. You can produce and promote a lot of music for the same price as placing a decent-size ad, and you will undoubtedly benefit more from the former than the latter.

Composers, agents, publishers, managers, etc., bombard the people who are in charge of choosing music for film and TV with information all the time. So, they really don't need to start thumbing through a magazine to find someone, nor do they have the time. *The Hollywood Reporter* produces several film music special editions where you will find various composers, record companies, and music publishers advertising, but this is usually a branding exercise rather than an attempt to solicit work.

On the other hand, generating publicity within those same pages is most definitely a good idea. Of course, it's not as simple to achieve as advertising (which is why many people simply opt for the easiest route and "pay for space"), but publicity is much more effective.

Most people—even in the business-to-business arena—don't

take too much notice of advertising, at least not to the degree they'd blindly believe whatever your ad stated. Everybody knows an ad exists only because someone paid for it, and it is therefore biased. Editorial, on the other hand, while undoubtedly reflecting the views of the writer, is at least considered impartial by many readers. If a journalist describes you as one of "Boston's most interesting new bands," while it may not sound like a glowing endorsement of everything you do, it is in fact much more valuable to you than an ad that announces you're "more talented than Lennon and McCartney."

Generating press coverage takes a lot of work and persistence. You'll need to identify publications, editors, and writers who are likely to cover your work and make sure that you get information about yourself and your work out to them. A thick skin is useful too, as the downside is that the impartiality of publicity can work against you if the writer decides to write something unfavorable.

Whether you're trying catch the attention of the press or market your skills to an industry executive, you'll need to make yourself comfortable with the following tools of the marketing trade:

Telephone
Probably the most intimidating method of communication when you are first marketing yourself, the telephone, also just happens to be about the most productive.

When you are speaking to someone, it is usually pretty apparent whether they are interested in what you are saying. If it is the first time you have spoken to them, they may not be too concerned about being especially friendly or polite to you, but that's okay, as you'll easily discover what they're really thinking.

The Cold Call
The cold call is a vital part of marketing yourself:

1. You can immediately ascertain the interest in yourself from the other party.
2. It provides an opportunity to build rapport.
3. It allows you to determine their personality type.

Voice Mail

What is it about voice mail that brings on such paranoia in so many people? One message…no call back. Two messages…no call back. By the third, you're imagination is running riot as to the reasons they haven't called. You could try phoning back at a different time each day—including outside traditional office hours when you may catch them unawares—but frankly it's quite likely the person you are trying to reach lets their calls go to voice mail all day.

To avoid this scenario, you need to give them a reason to call you back. If the reason in the first call doesn't work, then you give another one in your second call, and so on. Voice mail has at least one distinct advantage over other forms of communication—namely, you have sixty seconds to say whatever you want without interruption and the recipient is much more likely to listen for sixty seconds than they would be to read for sixty seconds.

This needs to be planned to some degree, otherwise if you're making a number of calls you'll easily forget what you said to each person. The hardest part is thinking of more than one reason why someone should call you back. So this is where you refer back to the USPs you established earlier in this chapter.

Here are some examples:

First Call

"Hi, this is Richard Jay. I understand you're the music supervisor for The Irish Priest *and you're looking for an adult contemporary ballad. I just wanted to let you know my band, Honeystone, has a couple of tracks which I believe may be suitable, and one of them is entitled "I Pray." I wanted to check I had your correct address and that the project was still open. I'd appreciate a quick call—my number is…"*

Hopefully you noticed the first USP in our example—a song title that's relevant to the theme of their project. Lyrics can be good USPs when pitching to specific projects as, if they cover similar topics to the film or TV program, they can really marry the music to the picture.

You may or may not get a call back. Either way, I suggest you mail the CD anyway: You weren't asking for permission, and at least now the recipient should remember your name.

Presuming you haven't received a reply to your first call—or within a week or so of your CD arriving—you make the second call:

Second Call

"Hi, this is Richard Jay calling regarding The Irish Priest. *I sent you a CD last week containing songs by Honeystone, including one called "I Pray." I just wanted to let you know their album was recently licensed to a major label in Japan, but we still control master and sync rights for all songs. I hope you enjoy listening to them and I'll speak with you soon. My number is…"*

This includes our second USP: The fact that we control master and sync rights. By stating this, I'm trying to establish the credibility of the band by informing my contact that a major label will be releasing the songs I have sent them; but at the same time I am reassuring them the deal with the label will not interfere with any licensing or soundtrack deal that may be offered. If the label owned the recordings outright or if there was a publisher involved who owned the copyright, then it is possible a deal could be blocked by either of them by demanding more money, moving slowly, or for any other reason. Where the artist or composer owns everything themselves, this would be far less likely to happen.

If the songs had been signed for release in the same country as the film was being released, then that would be another major USP: If the record was successful, the film would benefit—and vice versa. They would effectively be promoting each other.

The second phone call is a good time to give them your best shot: Your biggest USP. At this time, they should already have your music on their desk so if the USP works and piques their interest, then they don't have to look far to listen to the music. If, on the other hand, you had given them this information in the first call then they would have had to request the material from you and by the time it arrived they may well have forgotten why they asked for it in the first place.

If you still don't hear back, I'd give it a few more shots

depending upon how many USPs you have left. If you get a good review in a magazine, or are playing a gig near your contact, then mention it.

You may also want to try mixing and matching with some letter or e-mail strategies.

Contact Database

In my work as an industry consultant and broker, I'm in contact with literally thousands of people all around the world. Some of them I may only ever meet once or twice, e-mail a few times per year, and speak to even less. However, any one of them could be worth thousands of dollars to my business. So, how do I possibly keep track of everyone?

It goes without saying, I use a database where I collect everyone's contact details, areas of business, etc. But that alone isn't enough.

I have devised an extremely simple rating scheme that I apply to each of my contacts. It is a reflection of our relationship as it stands at a specific moment in time, and can therefore be changed whenever it is appropriate.

I assign each contact a letter between A and E:

A = High Potential / Approachable Personality
B = High Potential / Non-responsive
C = Low Potential / Approachable Personality
D = Low Potential / Non-responsive
E = Virtually No Potential

I should stress that a rating of *D* is in no way meant as a character assassination, or a slight against their people skills! It is merely an indicator of their personality type and a guide as to how they should be approached the next time you deal with them—by which time you may have otherwise forgotten your previous opinions of them.

If you do as I do and include this field in your database, you will be able to focus your marketing efforts much more effectively. For example, you may decide to keep in regular contact with your *A* list, but only contact your *B* list when you have a really good bit of news about yourself (such as just getting hired or licensed into a certain project). I have found *B* list contacts are often overworked and respond well to name-dropping or short e-mails/letters with important information in them. The *A* list, on the other hand, would normally respond well to more informal communication. Just because a contact is on the *A* list, doesn't mean they will never lose interest or forget you. Recently I saw a photo from someone on my *A* list in *Billboard* (unusual, because he lives in Hong Kong), so I sent a one-line e-mail informing him. It just so happened that at the time I was waiting for him to listen to some material I'd sent him. I'm sure my e-mail was appreciated more than a standard, "Have you listened yet?" message, yet had the same effect of reminding him of my submission.

People skills are one of the most important assets you can have in this industry. Music truly is a global business, and you will be dealing with people, cultures, and personalities that may seem alien to you. It is jokingly said that Britain and America are two nations divided by language, yet in reality they're of course culturally quite similar. Compare Japan with the U.S., or indeed Japan with China, and things start to get more difficult to compare.

In Japan, it can be considered quite intimidating to maintain eye contact with the person you are talking to. Yet in many Western countries, not maintaining eye contact could be considered rude or evasive. Whenever I attend trade fairs around the world, I often write comments on the plain reverse of people's business cards so I can remember our conversation. In Japan, this is seen as defacing their card and is regarded as a serious faux pas.

When speaking to someone whom you ultimately hope will pay for your music, first and foremost you want to make that person feel comfortable with you. Moderating our behavior to complement theirs is the most obvious way to accomplish this, as we all feel the most comfortable around those whom act as we do.

Some people may see this as manipulation, but I strongly disagree. How many of us would tell a rude joke when meeting our partner's mother for the first time? Or wear a T-shirt and jeans to a funeral of a respected elder?

We all restrict our behavior according to the situation we are in, and this is no different. Of course, all of the above is presuming you get to speak to the person you're after.

Letters and E-mail

Even using the above strategies, you may still not get a call back. I have found that people who seem totally unreachable by phone will often respond by e-mail. Certainly I tend to read and reply to my e-mail at times of the day when people wouldn't dream of phoning me; I also choose to do a certain amount of work on the weekend. I know there are many other people who work this way, so e-mails are an alternative approach when the voice mail isn't being returned *or* if the person you are calling is in a very different time zone from you. You may also find that people who aren't native English-speakers prefer a certain amount of communication in writing as it makes it easier for them to understand your message and reply to it.

With the speed of e-mail as compared to sending a letter, it is not surprising I recommend only sending a letter when it is accompanying something else—such as a CD or a signed contract—or as part of the direct-mail strategies below.

When you do send your CD, the letter should be short and sweet—for illustration purposes, my standard letter follows, but frankly, writing one is not exactly rocket science.

Also, don't be tempted to include numerous photos, a biography, press clippings, etc. I guarantee most of it will go in the garbage can without being read.

One useful tip when sending typed letters is to handwrite a P.S. at the bottom. These tend to get read before the rest of the text, so make sure whatever you write will make the recipient want to read your whole letter, and consequently listen to your music.

Incidentally, all of the suggestions made in the section dealing with voice mail strategies on the previous few pages also apply to letter writing.

The Music Broker Organisation

March 26, 2007

Dear Ms. Supervisor,

Please find enclosed a CD-R containing suggestions for *The Irish Priest.*

The Music Broker represents many catalogs from all over the world, covering everything from cutting-edge dance music to major artists from the 1960s. We hold exclusive rights in the masters, and in many cases, the publishing rights, too.

I hope the enclosed will be what you are looking for. But if it is not, please keep in touch and let me know what you're looking for next time.

Sincerely,

Richard Jay

Direct mail, whether it is by regular mail or e-mail, is a less personal, less specific but ultimately effective way of keeping your contacts informed of what you are doing. Consequently, it is used when you have already started to develop a relationship with a specific contact.

For example, if you have followed the advice already given, you'll have a list of contacts, some of whom (such as your *A* list) you will already have contacted.

Let's presume you've sent them a CD of your music, followed it up, and been told the material was good but not suitable for their current project. What now?

You need to ensure these people don't forget about you, as you may be perfect for their next project. What's more, you need to do it in such a way as to not appear to be "spamming" them or deluging them with junk mail.

As with the voice mail strategy, every time you make contact you should genuinely have something new to say. Good examples would include a postcard printed with the details of an upcoming gig or TV usage of your music. Alternatively, a favorable review in a magazine or even (re)launch of your Website will suffice.

Internet Promotion

While I remain decidedly skeptical about the Internet's supposed ability to create money for people out of thin air (as many people seem to believe), there is no doubt that it should be a major part of your overall marketing strategy.

First things first: The domain name. The various combinations of *www.firstnamesecondname.com* seem to have all but disappeared; indeed I was less than amused to discover not only that *www.richardjay.com* was already taken, but it belonged to someone who worked in music and entertainment whose full name is actually Richard Jay Alexander. Still worse, "Richard Jay," the Australian laundry equipment company, is always first in the search results for my name. I've had to settle for *www.richardjay.net* and hope that people looking for my music don't end up buying an industrial washing machine instead! So, don't make the same mistake I did: If your name is not taken, then claim it now and use it as your Internet home for all things musical.

Alternatively, you may have decided to form a company or have one already. You have a choice of naming your Website after your company name (such as *www.789music.com* for a company called 789 Music) or coming up with a clever Web address that describes an aspect of your business. My company's training division is at *www.Training4Music.biz,* and this kind of domain name probably generates more visits from sites like *www.google.com* than a more serious name like *www.trainingroom.com.*

The domain name is the equivalent of your front door. It allows people to meet and greet you easily. But you have to give them a reason to do so.

On the Web, content is king and varying the content on a regular basis is the best way to bring people back again and again. Some examples of this would include the obligatory "News" section where you can post updates on whatever is happening in your musical world. Additionally, you may find a public message forum or an online chat application would work. These have the added benefit of bringing interaction to your site so there is a two-way exchange of information (between yourself and your visitor). Realistically, it is unlikely that a music supervisor (or similar) will regularly surf into your chat room. You will probably find it will be the general public contributing the most—however when a potential user of your music goes to your Website, a busy site which has interaction between you and the fans of your music can only create a positive impression.

The biggest problem you may find initially though, is how to attract people to your site. Every possible way of attracting someone to your site can be put into one of two categories: Traffic you pay for and traffic you don't. Although a detailed look at Website promotion is beyond the scope of this book, I do want to give you an outline of the various things you can do to increase traffic.

First of all, your goal should be to get *targeted* traffic: There is no point in having five-hundred people at your site every day if most of them are looking for free MP3s by known artists. You're looking for quality, specific traffic. With that in mind, here are the main ways of creating that kind of audience:

Search Engine Submission

Once upon a time, in the dim and distant past of the mid 1990s, there were just a few million Web pages in the world. If you wanted to let people know about your Website you could submit its details to one of the fledgling search engines like Altavista or Lycos and be content in the knowledge that soon your details would be easily available to anyone who searched on your area of expertise. Those days, I'm afraid, are long gone.

With more than 325-million Websites in the world and a new one being created every four seconds, it is becoming increasingly difficult to make your presence felt on search engines. This doesn't mean that you shouldn't bother, it just means that it is only one part of your Website marketing strategy.

The most popular search engine, at least as I write this in Spring 2005, is Google. Not only is *www.google.com* the most visited site, but it also feeds other vitally important sites like AOL. So being listed at Google is your first priority and can be accomplished simply by clicking on their "About Google" link and following the submission instructions.

Other important engines to register with include Microsoft's MSN, Altavista, and Yahoo. Up until late 2004, many search engines were charging those who wanted to submit their site, or otherwise putting up barriers to try and reduce the number of further sites being listed on their engines. I would never recommend paying to be listed on a search engine: If you get listed on Google and follow some of the tips below, then you may very well end up being listed for free at those sites that wanted to charge you.

Links From Other Websites

When somebody new approaches me via the Internet, I always ask them how they found the Website: Nine times out of ten, they can't remember. The most likely reason for this is the very nature of Web surfing. You start off somewhere particular, and you just keep clicking from site to site until you find something of interest. For this reason, getting your Website listed on another site that already has a decent amount of traffic should be your next priority. They have already done a lot of hard work in generating traffic for their site and, as long as you only list on sites complimentary to your own, anyone that clicks through to your site is almost certainly going to be highly targeted. The other point to bear in mind is that most search engines keep a record of how many Websites have a link to your site. So, if you have listed yourself on one-hundred Websites and someone else is listed on only ten, then (all other things being equal) your site will be shown by Google before theirs.

So, when thinking about which sites you'd like to get listed on, start with you own list of favorites. Obviously, not every site will be prepared to list other people's sites, but quite a few will. Sometimes they will ask for a reciprocal link (where you must place a link from your Website to theirs).

E-mail Signatures

Once you have your Website created, you should make sure the address is at the bottom of every music-related e-mail you send out. It's possibly the easiest way of regularly putting your Web address in front of people. If you can come up with some kind of tagline that succinctly explains what you do, even better. For example, one of mine is:

Regards,
Richard Jay
—THE MUSIC BROKER NETWORK—
http://www.TheMusicBroker.net
"Hand-delivering the best unsigned talent to the heart of the entertainment industry"

Most e-mail programs and services let you create a signature that is automatically appended to the bottom of every outgoing e-mail, so this is one of those things you can set up and then never have to worry about.

You can take it one step further though. If you are active on any music-related Web forums, e-mail discussion lists, newgroups, etc., then include it as part of your signature there. As long as it is brief and relevant, nobody should complain about it.

Pay-Per-Click (PPC) Advertising

The main difference between this option and the previous ones is that this will cost you some money: Potentially quite a lot.

This is a form of advertising that only exists in the online world. To go back to my example of paying to advertise in something like *The Hollywood Reporter,* you'll recall that I advised against it unless you were happy to regard it as nothing more than a branding exercise. The problem with any kind of advertising is that it's too hit-or-miss. You pay a couple of hundred dollars for a pretty small part of a page and then hope that the kind of people you are after will buy the magazine, read your ad, *and* contact you. Unless all of those things happen, you have just wasted your money.

Pay-Per-Click works differently. If you start a PPC campaign, your ad will be shown free of charge to hundreds of thousands of people. Yes, that's *free of charge.* Not only that, but it will just be seen by people who are specifically searching on words and phrases that you determine are related to your Website. You only pay when somebody is interested enough that they actually click on your advertisement to visit your Website

The leaders in PPC are Google and Yahoo! Search Marketing (previously know as Overture). I'm a big fan of Google's search engine and likewise I think their Adwords service is the market leader. It allows you to pay as little as $0.05 per click, though you'll find that most of the words or phrases you'll be interested in will be around $0.30 or more.

Content

Music clips, will probably be the main reason why people are visiting—particularly if they are industry folk. They may be seeking a particular genre of music for a project they are working on, or maybe they are just looking at new composers and artists. Whatever the reason, you need to ensure there is something on your site for them. There are a number of ways this can be approached:

1. A short compilation of various pieces of music cut or segued together as a continuous piece.

In the real world, this would be known as a show reel. Psychologically this probably has an advantage, simply because the seamless editing of your music should guide the listener through all your best work without them having to navigate past long introductions or material which is inappropriate for them. On a show reel you can probably gamble by varying styles: Each piece would be so short the listener is likely to just "sit it out" rather than reach for the fast-forward button. A show reel of between five to eight minutes would be a good length, with up to a minute of each piece being common. The most common way of presenting this on your Website would be to encode it as a RealAudio or Windows Media file. Virtually every computer has one or both of these and they are long-established standards. You need software to create the files, but once that is done you don't need any special software on your site—just simply uploading the file and having a link to it from one of your pages is enough. You can find a current list of recommended software and Internet companies at *www.Training4Music.biz/resources.*

2. Pieces of music grouped by genre.

When your visitor knows the kind of material they are looking for, they'd probably appreciate having one page on your site where they could find, for example, all your world music tracks. Obviously, the disadvantage of this is if the visitor purely wants to get an overview of your work rather than one element of it; in this instance though, to keep everyone happy, you could have a show-reel page consisting of a world music show reel, an electronica show reel, etc. Again, I recommend simple links from each page to RealAudio and Windows Media files.

3. A searchable database of many different styles.

This approach is favored by company Websites—particularly business-to-business applications—and is best for those with large catalogs, such as music publishers, record companies, and music libraries. The idea is that all your sound files are linked to a database running on your Website. Each record in the database will contain details of your track and a hyperlink to the sound file. This record is searchable by the user so they can find a track that matches their exact criteria.

For example, let's say you have a track called "Indian Nights," which is a fusion of Indian music and contemporary dance rhythms. It has a tempo of 135bpm, is in the key of G minor, and features a female vocal singing in Urdu. All of this information (and anything else) can exist in the database record so a visitor to your site can search for all pieces of music at 135bpm, in the key of G minor, or featuring Indian/Urdu influences.

If you take a look at the home of my music publishing company, *www.burning-petals.com,* you can see an example of this. Obviously this solution is the most technically demanding of those described here, as you need much more than just links to RealAudio or Windows Media files. What you require is search engine software that can quickly find the most appropriate track for your visitor, much in the same way that Google finds the most appropriate Website for its visitor. Though complex, this solution is the most flexible and will occasionally prove itself extremely valuable to your visitors.

It is generally considered a good idea to collect at least the names and contact details of those who visit your site so you can keep in regular contact with them regarding your activities. At the very least, provide an opt-in mailing list where people can leave their name and e-mail address to receive further information by e-mail. You should also leave a space for "company name," but if someone leaves that blank you can often tell from their e-mail address whether they work for a company or not. So, if the address is *Bob.Giles@bobandjonmusic.com,* you would no doubt be making a visit to *www.bobandjonmusic.com* to see if they have a Website.

Sometimes, this approach won't work, as not every e-mail address has an associated Web address and people often have different e-mail addresses from that supplied by their employer.

Some sites go further and ask for address, phone/fax, type of business, etc. There is nothing wrong in doing this if the questions are well targeted, but bear in mind when filling out these kinds of forms, the boredom threshold is very low and the more you ask, the less inclined someone will be to fill out the form at all. Be sure to mark this information as optional and you shouldn't be doing too much harm.

So, once you have created your mailing list, what should you write to them about? First of all, you should regard this as a way of expressing your music and your personality. So, for example, if you are a classical composer, your communications would (likely) be much more formal than if you were an R&B artist. Your e-mails should set the tone for your music.

I recommend a quarterly newsletter to begin with. Monthly is going to be too often for most readers, unless you genuinely have a lot going on. Half yearly is not often enough. If you are a performing artist, you can fill your newsletter with details of upcoming performances, current releases (including those you are selling yourself), and any notable industry happenings such as airplay, record company showcases, and—hopefully—tracks licensed into film or TV.

A composer would have a slightly different-looking newsletter. If you are a composer of concert music, then you can make announcements of future performances and details of any releases that include your compositions. If you write for media only, then you should include announcements of past and future commissions.

All of that is fairly obvious, but if you really want your newsletter read rather than trashed I suggest you make it enter-taining to read. How far you go down that road is up to you, and again will partially depend on what style of music you are writing. Here, though, are some suggestions of things that will entertain your readership:

Other Artists/Composers: As counterproductive as it may sound, you may find that writing about other, similar artists or composers will be welcomed by the reader. Everyone who signed up for your newsletter is obviously interested in your style of music and therefore would be just as interested in similar music. I'm not saying you need to outright promote another artist, but you could have a few paragraphs each issue about artists that you've discovered and would recommend.

Opinion Pieces: If you have strong opinions on an aspect of music or film/TV, then feel free to include a short, well thought out discussion of it.

Your marketing strategy is an important part of your plan and often one that creative people find the most difficult. If you've ever listened to a piece of music and wondered why it was picked over the numerous other choices, I can virtually guarantee that on one level or another the answer is marketing. Though you may not like the thought of marketing yourself—few of us do—it is the only way to achieve prolonged success.

Take a look at *www.Training4Music.biz/resources* for more help and resources.

SIX

THE FIRST CONTACT

*R*egardless of what method you choose to use, sooner or later you will need to make a first impression on someone who is in a position to use your music or skills.

For the Composer/Musician

One of the main differences between composers and artists/song-writers is that the composer will often have to create new work for someone who they are pitching themselves to, whereas a band or artist is usually pitching finished tracks. This puts the composer in the unenviable position of trying to second-guess what somebody wants.

Either verbally, or in their opening letter, many composers make the mistake of claiming to be able to write every kind of music imaginable in the assumption that this is what the letter's recipient would want to hear the most. This is to be avoided at all cost, unless you truly are so gifted that no genre is beyond your talents. (Indeed, even if you are one of those blessed individuals, the chances are the person to whom you are promoting yourself will simply not believe you, so I would still think twice about it.) Whenever I hear a composer say those words, I conclude that I'm dealing with an amateur—an impression you should definitely avoid giving.

If a director chooses you to create a new piece of music for his project over somebody else, it is because he specifically liked an element of your work, as presented to him on your show reel. If he wanted a jazz score and he heard some jazz material of yours that he liked, your odds of being chosen have just increased dramatically. If he had to choose between someone who could write "anything" (and had a show reel crammed with every style under the sun) and someone who specialized in writing jazz (and had a reel to prove it)—who do you think would get the call first? Maybe it's a matter of opinion, but I think people generally trust the judgment of those who have dedicated themselves to one specific niche. Otherwise we'd all be hiring odd-job men to fix our houses, instead of specialists such as plumbers, carpenters, etc.

No, a much better idea is to specialize in a small number of styles and be the best you can be at those. Many of the great film composers have forged long, successful careers in this way—even the great Henry Mancini (who genuinely could turn his hand to most genres) was principally known, and hired, for certain styles.

Now I freely admit, the tricky part in this strategy is to ensure you don't lose touch with music users who don't immediately need your specialized styles of music. After all, the reason why people claim to be able to write everything is in the (false) belief this will somehow ensure they are at the top of every director's contact list whatever their projects requirements may be.

The best way around this is to avoid pigeonholing your musical output until you absolutely must. To the inevitable question of, "What kind of music do you write?" the best response would be that you specialize in a number of styles. Note the use of the word "specialize." This sets you apart from the jack-of-all trades, master-of-none brigade. This answer would often be sufficient to satisfy vague inquiries, but if the questioner is specifically seeking someone for a specific job, then you have to put yourself into salesperson mode. Answering a question with a question is a common but successful sales technique.

Maybe you write jazz funk music, but not traditional jazz; so when a director asks you whether you write "jazz" music, you need to establish which strand of the genre he is referring to. At this point, it is worth remembering he is seeking a composer because he (usually) is not a music professional. Therefore it is not a sensible idea to expect him to accurately distinguish between jazz funk and traditional jazz (as ridiculous as this may seem to jazz fans everywhere).

In all dealings with non-music people, try and use terms they, rather than you, are comfortable with. For example, an obvious start may be to ask him whether he is referring to the likes of George Benson, Jamiroquai, or Miles Davis. Things aren't necessarily that simple though. Maybe he has only heard of Jamiroquai or, worse still, he wants elements of all three (much worse could be asked of you, believe me). This is where you'll need to start being creative and conjure up some combination of abstract terms and reference points to find out what he really wants. There is no real substitute for sitting with a CD player and a large stack of various CDs, but until you get to that point, you should start using phrases such as:

- Are you looking for a dark score or something more upbeat?
- Is the story set in the past, present, or future?
- Are you looking for prominent music with strong melodies or do you want something more ambient?
- Should this character have a recurring theme?
- What do you want your audience to feel about this character?

Answers to these kinds of questions should point you in the right direction. Avoid terms that are so abstract they have no recognized meaning. You may know what you mean by "a green score with a touch of yellow," but most people won't have a clue.

For the Artist/Songwriter
For the artist/songwriter, specialization is even more the case. As you have just learned, the composer is principally a service provider so a certain amount of musical flexibility is a good thing. But the artist or songwriter, who is usually promoting their pre-existing work, can (and should) be as niche-oriented as they wish. In fact, some of the most frequently licensed artists are not the likes of Britney Spears and her multimillion-selling counterparts, but altogether more original, almost unique, artists.

Indeed, if you occupy a relatively small musical niche, your odds of being licensed are probably much greater than if you were producing "pure" pop music. Take an artist like Moby for example:

You won't hear his music on the radio too often, and many people may think they're not familiar with his work. But almost every track off his 1999 breakthrough album, *Play,* was used in film, TV, or advertising. Compare that to any of the big pop acts, who get far, far more radio airplay or record sales, and you may be surprised to find they are rarely chosen by film and TV departments.

Maybe these artists have been exposed in mass media enough already or maybe it's just that their music is not distinctive enough. Who knows?

In closing, let me ask you this: Would you rather be a big fish in a small pond or a small fish in a big pond? Most would prefer the former.

SEVEN

THE DEAL OFFER

You may be tempted to skip over the legal mumbo-jumbo in this chapter, in the belief that a good lawyer will take care of it for you. Well, a *good* lawyer would, but how would you even know a good lawyer when you met one if you don't know the first thing about music law? Additionally, the cost of appointing a lawyer (either good or bad) can often be greater than the money you earn from the agreement. Finally, as if that wasn't bad enough, it is not uncommon for lawyers to actually lose deals for their clients because they are too heavy-handed or inexperienced.

Early on in my career, when I first started working with a lawyer (a very well-known one, I might add) I asked for changes to an agreement I'd been given. I now realize that the changes I wanted were absolutely ridiculous and there was no way that we should have asked for them, but my lawyer simply said "Okay, I'll give it a go." The changes obviously weren't accepted. Fortunately, I didn't lose that deal, but I wouldn't have blamed the other party if they'd decided to withdraw their offer rather than work with someone who was apparently difficult or naïve.

Nobody will expect you to know the law inside out, but believe me, if you can confidently use terms like "work-for-hire" and "MFN," then you are in a much stronger position to negotiate an agreement without giving all your fee to a lawyer.

CASE STUDY NUMBER 1: COMPOSER

A national TV network is producing a new current affairs show. It is slated for a Sunday afternoon showing and is an in-depth look at a few of the big news stories of the week.

> They want:
> A 20-second opening theme
> A 30-second closing theme
> Various stings

A couple of other composers are being approached—including one who has worked closely with the director before—and they want everybody's free demos within two weeks from today.

CASE STUDY NUMBER 2: COMPOSER

A small, independent film company, whose work you are not familiar with, has heard your show reel and wants you to create both opening and closing titles and incidental music for their new feature film.

Their editor has created a temp track that they would like you to use as "inspiration" for the score. The film has no distribution, but they are likely to get it shown in film festivals, which they then hope will result in a distribution deal.

CASE STUDY NUMBER 3: ARTIST/SONGWRITER

A famous national TV network wants to use a song of yours for a new sitcom. It will be played in the background during a scene set in a bar.

They want "free TV" rights for the World for five years. The show is airing the day after tomorrow so they need an answer today.

CASE STUDY NUMBER 4: ARTIST/SONGWRITER

An indie film company in New York wants to use a song of yours over the end titles of their new film, but they would like you to remove the lead vocal from the first verse.

They want "all" rights and "video/DVD buyout" for the World in perpetuity. They also hope to release a soundtrack album and want your "in principle" agreement to that, pending further negotiations "in good faith" at a later date.

These are very typical examples of offers that may be made to an artist/songwriter or a composer with a few credits behind him. You can see the timeframes are pretty short, so even though you most probably don't have an offer for your music right now, it is a good idea to study this chapter now so you will be able to think clearly when the phone call does come in.

First and foremost, the average person will want to know what their fee is. There's absolutely nothing wrong with money being a major reason why you work. Do you think the teller at your local bank is doing their job purely out of love for banking? It is wise though, to not appear totally money driven if your contact is responsible only for the creative decisions instead of the business or financial ones.

As we discussed earlier, different people are responsible for different tasks on a project. The bigger the project, the greater the number of people involved. In my experience, a film's director is normally more creative than the producer, but this is not always the case. It is best you establish as soon as you can who has the final say on music matters.

What's In It for the Composer?

The kind of financial deals offered to composers—particularly by low-budget projects—are surprisingly varied and often confusing. Let's take a look at some typical fee examples.

Straight Fee

This is the simplest arrangement. Typically, the composer would be paid a fee—probably in two or three installments—and the commissioner would be granted (in writing) the necessary rights to legally use the music they have commissioned. Ideally, no other rights would be granted by the composer, so the commissioner would need to go back to the composer and make further payments for additional use. In Case Study Number 2, the composer was told the film was likely to be exhibited at festivals (such as Sundance or Cannes), so they definitely need to be granted permission to use the composer's work for a limited festival run.

The composer's performing rights must always be retained so that they can be assigned to a PRO. It is not uncommon for an inexperienced filmmaker to ask for the composer's performing rights. That is completely unnecessary and if the composer is already a member of a PRO, he does not, in fact, own the performing rights in his work. By joining a PRO you are giving your performing rights to the PRO so that they can collect the accrued royalties on your behalf. This is an exclusive assignment so you cannot assign them to anyone else at the same time.

If possible, the composer should retain the rights for TV, theatrical release (i.e., cinema), sell-through (VHS/DVD, etc.), and other forms of commercial usage.

Note that I say "if possible:" Not surprisingly, the commissioner, if he is sufficiently knowledgeable about such matters, will want to take as many rights as he can, even if he doesn't anticipate using those specific rights. However, this does tend to vary from country to country. For example, much TV and feature film commissioning in the U.S. is done under the "work-for-hire" agreement that is part of the U.S. Copyright Act. This typically assigns many rights to the commissioner, up to and including the entire copyright, allowing them to use the music in whatever media they see fit and in whatever way they wish.

In other countries, it simply comes down to the negotiation skills of each party. In situations like Case Study Number 2, the money on offer is normally so low the composer is in a better bargaining position on contractual matters. At the end of negotiations, you need to be happy with the money received as compared to the rights granted.

One extra thing to bear in mind is before getting the deal, the commissioner may expect you to prepare a demo free of charge. It is my opinion there are more deserving charities than multimillion-dollar TV networks, but sadly the proliferation of affordable home-recording equipment has led to the oversupply of composers. Consequently there are many who are willing to demo for free in the hope of getting the job. At least get them to pay the tape or courier costs so you don't take a loss.

Deferred Payment or Profit Sharing

Sometimes the commissioner will offer the composer a share of the film's future profits in order to compensate him for the low—or even non-existent—fee. I can say that I would never agree to score a low-budget film on that premise, but I concede there are valid reasons for agreeing to this, such as "building" your show reel and résumé.

However, if you do agree to profit share, do it in the belief you will never get paid any money for your work.

The odds of a typical feature film making a reasonable profit are so small as to be comparable to your chances of winning the lottery—probably worse. There are too many variables to consider for it to be a good idea. For example, how many other people are on profit share and how many are being paid an upfront fee? In the case of the latter, their fees are "costs," so someone else is being paid while you're still waiting for the film to turn a profit.

If you absolutely must agree to this and ever hope to see any money, at least make sure you agree on exactly what constitutes profit. You can easily do this by agreeing to a basic list of the various costs involved in the making of the project. Maybe once you've seen just how many other people are being paid upfront, you will be less inclined to gamble on the film being profitable.

A better option would be where you are guaranteed a fixed fee in the future if the project reaches a certain milestone: For example, a distribution deal is signed or the film grosses a specific amount at any time in the future. Unlike profit, gross figures are much easier to agree on and, therefore, much less likely to cause problems or misunderstandings later on.

Bear in mind though, if you agree to this, the total fees you get over the period of the project should equal more than if you had just agreed to a larger fee upfront. For example, if you agree you will receive a second payment upon them securing a distribution deal, you would have more than likely only granted limited rights in return for the first payment. When factoring the amount of the second payment, do not simply agree to the figure you would have charged on day one as this does not take into account the risk you are taking in waiting for a future payment. You should probably put your banker hat on and decide what kind of interest rate you want to charge. Adding a further 50% of the fee, for example, would not be unreasonable.

What's In It for the Artist/Songwriter?

The straight fee is the simplest arrangement. Indeed, it is usually simpler to license pre-existing music than new commissions, even if the music publisher and record company own the rights.

Typically, the fee agreed is paid in one lump sum by the film or TV company ("Licensee") to the copyright holder ("Licensor"), and as before, they are granted either the minimum amount of rights necessary for their project *or* they pay much more for additional rights.

In my experience, it is more rare for the artist/songwriter to be offered a deferred payment or profit share deal than it is for the composer: Ironic, considering the former is risking very little by licensing a pre-existing work.

The only situation where the two are comparable is Case Study Number 4, in which the licensee requires revisions. In this instance, you will be incurring expenses to provide a custom-made mix to the licensee that is unlikely to be of use to you outside of the project. It is not at all unreasonable, therefore, to charge a higher fee. However, to make life easier for yourself in the future, you may want to get in the habit of always producing instrumental mixes of your tracks. In the event someone wants a mix without vocals, you can either charge them a lower fee or charge them the same fee but not be required to spend any more of your time preparing the mix.

"Most Favored Nations" Clause

You'll like this. I almost couldn't believe such a thing could be applied to music licensing when I first heard about it.

Negotiating a price for a license is a tricky proposition. If you go too low and discover other people were paid more, you're not going to be too happy. Go too high on the other hand, and you may lose the whole deal. Wouldn't it be great if the licensee had to treat you the same way he'd treated most of, if not all, the other licensors?

Well that's exactly what an MFN (most favored nations) clause is. It has existed in one form or another since the late nineteenth century and, as the name suggests, was principally used between nations: Initially Asia and Western countries, but now includes virtually everybody except a few "rogue" nations.

Naturally you don't get this benefit automatically, but when negotiating, if you feel there's significant room for maneuvering, then simply say you want to "MFN with all the other licensors." In other words, get paid the same as everyone else.

> They may object. Their objection may be that your track (for example) is in the background, and over the end titles is a Gold-selling artist. In this case, you agree to MFN with all tracks except titles and any Gold-selling artist.

Use

One thing which is important to bear in mind is the way in which the music will be used in the project, as this is directly related to its value—for both licensee and licensor.

Types of Use

For example, in Case Study Number 4, the song is required for the end titles. In other words, there will be no on-screen action and no dialogue when the music is played. This is one of the most expensive uses and attracts the highest price tag.

Conversely, Case Study Number 3 involves a song being played in the background of a sitcom during a scene set in a bar. For starters, sitcoms aren't known for being a genre that relies heavily on music—unlike drama, for example. So straight away you should realize the music is very much playing a supporting role. More importantly though, it is unlikely anyone will be able to hear much of the track under the sound effects from the bar. This will definitely result in a much lower fee being offered than for main or end titles.

It's also worth checking exactly how your music is going to be used in the project, as you may find it objectionable or alternatively, feel you should be paid a higher fee.

For example, I once heard of a film that climaxed with music written by a rock star who had committed suicide. It was being played over a scene of the film's main character attempting suicide. At this point in the film, the camera pans to show a poster of the rock star on the character's wall. Only after this had been filmed did the music supervisor apply for a license to the record company and music publisher. When the former found out how the music was intended to be used, their reply was a resounding and complete refusal to license the music at all, presumably on the grounds of decency. The filmmaker was forced into re-shooting the scene at immense cost.

Alternatively, you may find the dialogue of a scene is almost identical to the theme of your song's lyric. The chances of the licensee finding another song that fits so precisely would be very small, so you'd be justified in asking for a higher fee in this instance. If the project had the same name as your song, then you may really be onto a money-spinner...but bear in mind it is much easier to change the name of a project than to re-shoot one scene, so don't be too greedy.

Number of Uses

While it is not the norm for a song to be used more than once in a project, it's not entirely unusual either. Obviously, this results in a higher fee to the licensor—though it is rarely an additional 100% for each additional use—and the performance royalties will also usually be doubled as they are paid per use. Charging a licensee on the basis of how many times the music is used is often known as "needledrop."

Length of Each Use

Some licensors, particularly those outside of North America, license on the basis of length rather than on a needledrop basis. Sometimes it is based on a unit of thirty seconds—so a usage of thirty-two seconds would be twice as much as thirty seconds. Note that this does not affect performance income in the same situation, which is paid according to the actual usage and sometimes the exact length. The PRO doesn't care what master licensing arrangements you made.

Rights

In the beginning there was only one way to see either a film or TV show, namely by going to the movies or turning on your TV. Over the past thirty years though, we've had such technological advances as cable, video, laserdisc, CD-ROM, DVD, Internet, video-on-demand, and many others. So what does this have to do with music licensing?

Well, as we've seen, when a piece of music is licensed or commissioned, rights have to be granted for its legal use, and it is normal to specify what media the music can be incorporated in.

Rather than try and see into the future, music companies have come up with a number of phrases that describe different kinds of media or exhibition. Not all terms are used in all countries.

Festival Rights

Most low-budget films only require permission from the owner to use their music in film festival exhibitions. Many such films were created to draw attention to the director or scriptwriter, rather than to be a viable commercial film. Consequently, a festival rights license often stipulates that no profit should come from the exhibition of the film—or if it does, then a further payment must be made to the copyright owner. If the filmmaker thinks there is a strong chance of his film having a life outside of the festivals, but he cannot afford to pay for further rights now, he could negotiate a step deal where he pays only for the rights needed at any one time, but agrees to future fees in the event of further rights becoming necessary. This is an advantage to the filmmaker, since they would normally be required to obtain a new license at whatever rate the licensor decides. If the film had been successful since the first license was negotiated, the licensor would no doubt charge considerably more when the filmmaker required further rights.

Theatrical Rights

These are simply the right to include specific pieces of music in a film intended to be shown in cinemas (only).

Free TV Rights

As most feature films progress from cinema to pay-TV, free TV rights normally apply only to shows made purely for network transmission. "Free" in this instance refers to any channel that does not require a subscription fee, such as ABC, CBS, or NBC.

Video/DVD Buyout

To avoid having to enter into future negotiations with each of the music copyright holders, most films will wish to negotiate the right to include the music in future VHS or DVD releases at the outset. They will most likely ask for a buyout of your rights, rather than agree to a royalty per unit sold. It is typical for a buyout to cost between 75% and 100% of your initial license fee, so when the licensee is dealing with a tighter budget you may get a per unit royalty instead.

Broad Rights/All Media

This covers most of the rights that are typically required, such as festival, free TV, theatrical, pay/subscription TV, cable TV, and a video/DVD buyout. It does not cover certain rights such as publishing or soundtrack albums, which must be separately licensed.

Territory

The territory of a license is the country (or countries) that are covered by the agreement. Invariably, the licensee will require the 'World' or the 'Universe' (for we can't say for sure whether at some point in the future people will be watching from somewhere in space...). It is up to you to decide whether you're happy to license the world for the amount of money they are offering, and if you're not happy then try to exclude some territories. Excluded territories can always be subject to negotiation later, for an additional fee.

Term

The term of a license is simply the amount of time until the agreement between the licensee and licensor expires. Again, the licensee wants as long as possible, but the compromise term is usually five years. The licensee may then ask for a clause in the license where both parties agree at the outset what fee will be charged in the event the licensee wants to renew the license before its expiration. This is known as an option.

Publishing Rights

Aside from the rights you grant the project to use your music, it is unfortunately becoming increasingly common for them to seek your entire publishing rights also. There can be few reasons why you would wish to do this, but the most likely is that the makers of the project will simply withdraw the commission from you unless you agree to their request.

What makes this practice somewhat laughable though, is many of the film and TV companies that want your publishing rights are not actually bona fide music publishers or members of a PRO and consequently, have no way to collect the money that becomes due.

A more extreme example of this practice is where one or more people involved in the project ask to be listed as co-writers of the music so they can benefit from the income generated by your work. Frankly, if this is suggested to you, then you should flatly refuse. It is actually against the rules of most performing-rights organizations for someone to be listed as a co-writer when they did not contribute to the composition. More than that though, it is an extremely objectionable way for someone to do business with you and if your refusal leads them to work with another composer in the future, then I don't believe you've lost a great contact.

Copyright

Let me draw your attention to a rather important phrase in Case Study Number 2:

> *"Their editor has created a temp track that they would like you to use as 'inspiration' for the score."*

The temp track will consist of work by other composers or artists that your contact hopes will "inspire" your work. In truth, what they are suggesting is that each piece of music you write bears a strong resemblance to each piece in their temp track. They are looking for a sound-alike.

The problem in these cases, which are all too common, is the person taking all the risk is, in fact, the composer.

Invariably, the editor or director has filled up their temp track with all their favorite artists and songs—material which would be prohibitively expensive to license—and now they are looking to find someone to replace the dummy soundtrack with material that sounds very close to the originals, both in melody and production.

The best-case scenario is the composer does a great job, the producer and director are happy, and the composer doesn't get sued. The worst-case scenario is the composer does a great job, the producer and director are happy, but the composer gets sued for a huge sum.

You see, whichever way you look at it, the loser in this scenario is the composer—nobody else. Composers have gone bankrupt after being successfully sued for copyright infringement. The ironic part is the claimant in a case like this would be the composer's client (the production company). The music publisher would have sued the production company for infringement; the production company would then have the right to sue the composer, as the contract between composer and client states quite clearly he must write an original work.

If you must take on a job like this, then you need to be absolutely sure you will not be infringing copyright by staying too close to the original temp track. This is harder than you might think as the late ex-Beatle George Harrison found when he was accused of directly copying The Chiffons 1963 hit *He's So Fine* and turning it into *My Sweet Lord* (1970). The court found in favor of the song's publisher, but acknowledged that Harrison may not have deliberately copied the song. Nonetheless, it was still ruled as infringement.

A safer option, and one which the composer might be able to convince the filmmaker into choosing, is to do cover versions of the songs in question. Here's how it works:

1. Ordinarily, to use a song in a film, both a sync and master license would need to be obtained from the music publisher and record company, respectively.

2. Your total cost would be much reduced if you avoid using the original record company master and recreate it with new musicians and singers. The master license is normally more expensive than the sync license, because publishers benefit from future royalties (such as performance) which the record company does not.

3. Therefore, the filmmaker should first make a request to the music publisher for a sync license and once it has been granted, the composer can recreate the original recording at a

much lower cost. Alternatively, there are companies who specialize in recreating masters—sometimes involving the original "out-of-contract" performers—and they may already have a suitable version of the required song. Mimicry is not illegal—though it's rarely satisfying from a creative point of view. Copying music and passing it off as your own work is definitely illegal.

Royalties

Aside from the initial payments for your work, there are also a number of other possible income streams to be aware of.

If you happen to be involved with a low-budget project, the commissioner will be eager to point out the low fee they are paying will be more than offset by the performance royalties you will receive for the broadcast of your work. Indeed, it's becoming increasingly common for some production companies to offer no fee at all and use this as their argument.

While it is true PRO income can be sizable, it unfortunately cannot—and should not—be relied upon. Performance royalties are paid by movie theaters in most countries, but not in the U.S. Outside of America, movie theaters are required to pay either a percentage of the ticket price or a set fee per theater seat. Depending upon the kind of project you are working on, this would be an important source of income.

The next biggest area of PRO income is TV. Allocating money to all the writers of all the music used on TV worldwide is obviously a mammoth task. It isn't surprising therefore that not every society makes a perfect job of it. Consequently, a PRO statement resembles something of a lottery.

You should allow at least a year for payment from national broadcasts—two or three years for international—and only then will you have any idea as to whether you have been properly compensated. In the U.S., things are further complicated by the existence of three different PROs (ASCAP, BMI, and SESAC), of which a writer/composer can only belong to one. They each pay according to different calculations, even for the same use, so deciding which one to join is an important decision.

Not only that, but the type of use and whether the music is with or without vocals also drastically affects the amount of money paid in certain territories—again, the U.S. being one of the worst culprits for this. Broadly speaking, although the broadcaster is "charged" the same for both vocal and instrumental music, and featured and background usages by the PROs, vocal music is paid at a higher rate than instrumental, and featured use (where you can clearly hear the music) is paid at a higher rate than background use. This is despite the fact that, on average, 90% of music in film or TV is instrumental and used in the background behind dialogue and sound effects. In the preparation of this book, I contacted all three U.S. PROs asking them to explain this policy: None of them replied.

Confusing, isn't it? Discount any future performance income from any fee negotiations with a commissioner and treat royalties as a bonus.

Secondary Usage

Beyond the TV set or cinema, there is considerable money to be made if a project containing your music is sold on DVD or VHS.

The feature-film market can sell in the region of 15- to 20-million copies of a blockbuster, but even the so-called "art house" sector can sell significant numbers of key films. The popularity of TV series' on DVD/VHS has increased over recent years and income here may even surpass that from the original usage.

There are a number of ways in which you will be compensated for this usage, but payment relies on you not having given up all rights and/or publishing rights in your initial negotiation. Of course, it is possible you were made a good financial offer that tempted you to do just that, but on the whole it is best to give away the minimum amount of rights possible.

Soundtrack albums have been around for decades now and many have proved to be successful. It is undoubtedly true though, that albums consisting of purely incidental music are far less successful than those containing songs. Indeed, it seems to hardly matter whether the songs on the soundtrack album were ever actually in the film.

When negotiating an agreement to use a piece of music in a film that is expected to have a soundtrack album, this subject will more than likely be brought up at an early stage by the licensee. This is for two reasons: They need to ensure you are broadly in agreement with the idea (i.e., will negotiate at a later date in "good faith") and they may ask you to reduce your license fee in consideration of the extra income you would receive from a soundtrack album. This is usually acceptable: A 10% reduction of the fee would be typical.

If you are a performing artist, you may also find that usage in film and TV increases the interest in your music from publishers and labels wishing to capitalize on the newfound public awareness of your music. As noted in the introduction to this book, many artists have benefited from this, so if you do find yourself involved in a successful project, make sure you use some of the marketing strategies in Chapter Five, Marketing Yourself, to keep those fickle A&R departments interested!

EIGHT

CONTRACTS AND COMPLETING THE DEAL

*E*verything explained in the previous chapter would have been informally discussed between licensor and licensee before it came time to write everything down. It is important, for a number of reasons, that both parties are clear on what has been agreed to *before* the license agreement is drawn up.

If one party receives a contract from the other which has something not previously agreed, they may think they were deliberately not told about it in the hope they wouldn't notice. If either party is using a lawyer, any misunderstandings or confusion will push their legal fees up. Finally, if you do end up requesting a change to a clause the licensee felt you'd already agreed to, it could easily make you look unprofessional and difficult.

Presuming the licensor and licensee have discussed the matter and agreed on the points, the first thing the licensee would require is these key points in writing, signed by the licensor. Until the full agreement is signed, this letter is legally binding on both parties and is particularly necessary where there is no time to prepare a full agreement before the inclusion or transmission of your music. This document is known as the short form or deal memo. Whoever generates the agreement, be it the licensee or any of the licensors (which could include record company, music publisher, or in the case of an unsigned artist, the individual themselves) there are certain things that must be included.

Sample Publisher Letter of Agreement

Date: *July 1, 2005*
To: *Paddy O'Donnell*

Further to our recent discussions, I have pleasure in confirming the terms of the license agreed by us, as follows:

Title of Composition: *In My Heart*
Writer(s)/Composer(s): *Richard Jay*
Artist: *Honeystone*

Project Title: *The Irish Priest*
Project Synopsis / Scene Description: *The film is the life story of an Irish priest who has emigrated to Boston. The above song is featured in the love scene between the priest's character and his girlfriend.*

Type of License: *Synchronization*
Type of Use: *End Titles*

Licensor/Publisher: *Burning Petals Music Ltd.*
Principal Contact: *Richard Jay*
Licensee: *Green Shamrock Films*
Principal Contact: *Paddy O'Donnell*

Number of Uses: *1*
Length of each Use: *63 seconds*
Type of each Use: *Background*

Territory: *World*   **Term:** *Perpetuity*

Rights Granted: *Festival Rights and Theatrical Rights*
Agreed License Fee: *$15,000.00 (U.S.)*

Yours sincerely,   Read and Agreed by:

Richard Jay   Paddy O'Donnell
On behalf of   On behalf of
Burning Petals Music Ltd.   Green Shamrock Films

Sample Record Company Letter of Agreement

Date: *July 1, 2005*
To: *Paddy O'Donnell*

Further to our recent discussions I have pleasure in confirming the terms of the license agreed by us, as follows:

Title of Composition: *In My Heart*
Writer(s)/Composer(s): *Richard Jay*
Artist: *Honeystone*

Project Title: *The Irish Priest*
Project Synopsis / Scene Description: *The film is the life story of an Irish priest who has emigrated to Boston. The above song is featured in the love scene between the priest's character and his girlfriend.*

Type of License: *Master Use*
Type of Use: *End Titles*

Licensor/Record Company: *Burning Petals Music Ltd.*
Principal Contact: *Richard Jay*
Licensee: *Green Shamrock Films*
Principal Contact: *Paddy O'Donnell*

Number of Uses: *1*
Length of each Use: *63 seconds*
Type of each Use: *Background*

Territory: *World*   **Term:** *Perpetuity*

Rights Granted: *Festival Rights and Theatrical Rights*
Agreed License Fee: *$15,000.00 (U.S.)*

Yours sincerely,   Read and Agreed by:

Richard Jay   Paddy O'Donnell
On behalf of   On behalf of
Burning Petals Music Ltd.   Green Shamrock Films

If an unsigned artist who represents both master and sync rights was preparing the paperwork, he could either present two documents (such as these two) or simply amalgamate the information into one.

Some licensors like to include language stating this is a temporary, but nonetheless, legally binding agreement, that is in lieu of a main agreement known as the long form. Regardless of whether it has this statement or not, it is important to remember that whatever you agree to on the short form, you must agree to on the long form.

You may also wish to cover yourself by stating that rights are only conferred upon payment of the specified fee, otherwise a licensee with a slow accounts payable department may have the legal right to use your music when you haven't received your money.

Long Form Agreement

These can typically run to at least three or four pages, so to try and lower your legal fees (and increase your knowledge), I'm going to give you my interpretation of certain boilerplate clauses that are in general use around the English-speaking music world. First though, I need to give you a really big disclaimer:

> **REALLY BIG DISCLAIMER**
> I am not a lawyer, and would never wish or claim to be one. What follows is purely my interpretation and opinions. I strongly suggest you do not act on this information alone, but seek out qualified legal advice. I will absolutely not be held liable for any losses.

A long form license agreement usually starts like any other contract. It states the date the parties entered into the agreement, along with their legal names and addresses. Next, it would specify the name of the piece of music being licensed, its performer, the name of the film or TV show, uses, territory, and term (all as previously agreed in the short form).

Rights

The first clause we will look at (usually on page one of any agreement) is clarification of exactly which rights are being granted.

> *Licensor hereby licenses and grants to Licensee (which expression shall include its licensees successors and assignees) the non-exclusive right to record the Composition or any part thereof in timed synchronization with the Picture throughout the Territory.*

The music copyright holder is the Licensor and the party wishing to use it (such as the film company or TV station) is the Licensee. In this clause, the Licensor is allowing this specific company and anyone else this company has a legal relationship with, to include the specific piece of music ("Composition") in a specific film/show (named elsewhere in the agreement) anywhere in the Territory. By stating it is a non-exclusive right, the Licensor clarifies they are able to license the same track to anyone else they want, without permission from the Licensee. In other words, no transfer of copyright has taken place.

Performance Rights
(Not To Be Confused With Performing Rights)

> *Licensor further grants to Licensee the non-exclusive right to sell, distribute, and export copies of the Composition and Publicly Perform for Profit said Composition throughout the Territory but only in timed synchronization with the Picture.*

The Licensee is being given permission to allow public viewing of the project containing the composition, such as in a movie theater or by TV transmission (according to whether the Licensee has been granted theatrical or TV rights elsewhere in the agreement). They are also allowed to sell or export the project, such as on DVD/VHS or by licensing their master tapes to other film distributors or TV stations. Without this clause, the Licensee would be unable to profit from their project outside of their own country and would also be unable to show it on TV stations owned by other companies (for example).

Obligations, Warranties, and Guarantees

This next example is from a U.K. contract and applies equally to pre-existing songs that are licensed and new commissions whose copyright is assigned. You will find almost identical wording in license agreements worldwide, not just in the U.K. It deals with the obligations or "warranties" on the Licensor:

The Licensor hereby warrants and represents that:

a. *The Composition is an original and unencumbered copyright work and the exploitation by the Licensee hereunder will not violate or infringe the rights of any third party;*

b. *The Licensor has full right and power to assign the rights herein assigned and such rights are free and clear of any claims, demands, liens, or encumbrances;*

This is an important clause as it deals with the guarantees the Licensor is making to the Licensee: Namely, the composition is wholly original and written by the specified individual(s). Additionally, the Licensor is guaranteeing he knows of no legal issues surrounding the composition, such as an infringement claim. The Licensee needs this confirmation because they could unintentionally be infringing copyright if they licensed a track from someone who it later turned out was not the (only) copyright holder.

In certain countries, particularly European ones, you may also find a clause relating to so-called "moral rights." Moral rights cover two basic issues: The right of the composer to be identified as the author of the composition ("paternity") and the ability to object to derogatory treatment of the composition ("integrity"). Unless the composition is created under an employment or "work for hire" agreement, the rights cannot be assigned to anyone else, so they always remain with the composer rather than a publisher. They can, however, be waived and composers are frequently asked to do so by a publisher.

The reason for this is the commissioner does not want the rights—particularly integrity rights—used against them in law. For example, the composer may object to the visuals of the project that is using their music and attempt to use the right of integrity to have it removed.

In the U.K., moral rights are covered under the 1988 Copyright Designs and Patents Act. Moral rights are not recognized by any specific law in the U.S., even though it signed on to the 1971 Berne Convention which introduced them. The U.S. claims it complies with its obligations by virtue of a number of pre-existing laws, such as defamation, unfair competition, and the derivate right under its copyright law. Regardless of whether that is accurate or not, they certainly do not have specific regulations like many of the other Berne signatories.

Master Use

Of course, it is only fair the licensee also make certain guarantees. This is an example clause from a master use license:

> *Licensee warrants and agrees that Licensee will obtain in writing all necessary consents and permissions of the copyright owners of the Composition for the synchronization and performance of the Composition. Licensee shall be solely responsible for and shall pay all moneys required to be paid to the copyright owner of the Composition recorded in the Master for the synchronization and performance of the Composition in the Picture and all so called "re-use" and similar fees required to be paid in connection with the recording of the Master in the Picture.*

The Licensee is agreeing to get a license from the copyright holder of the music and words, as well as this license for the recording, and is acknowledging they are solely responsible for payments to the publisher. Having the right to use just the recording is not enough—permission must also be sought from the publisher.

Of course, dealing with two different rights holders can cause problems, such as if the record company agrees but the publisher doesn't (or wants too much money). Given the fact that you cannot license any piece of music without the permission of the publisher—even if the record company does give permission—it makes sense for a Licensee to approach the publisher first, knowing that if a deal is struck they would at least be able to license another version of the same song if the record company refused to license the specific recording the licensee wanted.

The "re-use" fee, sometimes known as the "new use" fee, is a payment that needs to be made to the American Musicians Union (AFM) when music for a film is released as a soundtrack album. If the music was not recorded under union rules, then this does not apply.

It is interesting to note the Licensee never guarantees to actually use the music they have licensed/commissioned, but they do guarantee to pay for it.

Indemnification

Indemnification is one of the key points in any agreement and ideally each party should indemnify each other.

> *Licensee will indemnify and hold Licensor harmless from any and all claims, damages, costs, demands, and expenses (including reasonable legal fees and costs) arising out of or in connection with any breach of Licensee's warranties, representations, or covenants under this agreement, or in any way resulting from or connected with Licensee's unauthorized use of the recording.*

Basically, the Licensee is protecting the Licensor from any legal or financial problems which arise through the Licensee intentionally or unintentionally breaking its guarantees in this agreement. If that sounds unusually generous, remember that you are invariably required to do at least the same for them.

So, the indemnification clause essentially backs up everything that has already been said—such as the work being original—and further agrees that if any of it is found to have not been true or ignored during the term of the agreement, that party (Licensee or Licensor) which guaranteed the clause will be responsible for the consequences. Furthermore, it also applies if a clause is under dispute. For example, where a commissioning contract (which, remember, also gives the copyright in the new music to the commissioner) calls for an original work, if a third party accuses the composer of plagiarism and decides to take the commissioner to court, it would be the composer who stands to potentially lose a lot of money.

Jurisdiction

Jurisdiction is one of those clauses that many people don't pay too much attention to. It simply states which country's law will apply in the event of one party wishing to take the other to court. As someone who has entered into agreements with companies overseas which have turned out to not be worth the paper they're written on, let me assure you that if you have to sue someone in a foreign country under foreign laws, you have a big problem.

> *This agreement shall be governed by and construed in accordance with English law and the parties agree to submit to the jurisdiction of the Courts of England and Wales.*

Of course, anyone who has ever been down this road will know the importance of jurisdiction so they'd be highly unlikely to agree to your country's law being solely applicable. Fortunately, there is a solution in so-called joint jurisdiction. This provides for the agreement to be subject to a certain country's law but also allows one of the parties to instigate legal proceedings in another country. I'm not sure how common this alternate clause is as I've had a few confused comments from people over the years, but it is certainly something to be aware of if you feel you have the power to negotiate.

Resources

Below, I've listed answers to some of the most common questions I am asked. In addition, I've included my personal choice of resources. As these are constantly being updated, please refer to *www.Training4Music.biz* for more information.

Frequently Asked Questions
Who owns "your" music?
You own the copyright in the music and/or words unless you have signed a publishing deal and therefore assigned the ownership of your rights to the publisher.

You own the copyright in the recording unless somebody else has paid the associated costs (such as studio time, musician, etc.) or you have signed a recording contract/exclusive licensing contract and therefore assigned the rights to a third party.

You own the performing rights unless you have joined a performing-rights organization and therefore assigned the ownership of your performing rights to the organization.

Why is this important?
Only the copyright holder can license the publishing and/or master rights. So if you do not own the music you have created, you may have no legal control over it (depending upon the exact terms of your contract).

Conversely, if you do own the rights, then there is nothing to prevent you from entering into any licensing agreement you wish—

including giving your music away. Potential licensees know this and regard self-ownership as a good thing, as long as the copyright holder knows how to conduct business.

Will licensing music to a film or TV show cause problems if I later want to sign a record or publishing deal?
Ninety-nine percent of licensing deals are non-exclusive, which means they place absolutely no restrictions on your future ability to permanently assign or grant your rights to a third party.

Glossary

A&R: An abbreviation for Artist & Repertoire, it is a record company department responsible for signing new artists, looking after the current roster, and finding suitable songs for any non-writing artists.

Advance: Money paid upfront to a licensor before royalties are actually collected. This money is deducted from the royalties as they accrue until the licensee has fully recouped (i.e., received royalties equal to the amount already advanced) at which point the licensor begins to receive royalties.

All Media: An all-encompassing group of the most requested rights including festival, free TV, theatrical, pay/subscription TV, cable TV, airlines, ships, and video/DVD buyout. Other rights, such as those for a soundtrack release, would be negotiated separately.

Assignment: The process of legally transferring rights to another person or entity on a permanent basis.

Background Use: Refers to the prominence of a piece of music in a film or TV show. If it is classed as "background," then it is usually below dialogue or sound effects, possibly to the point of almost being inaudible.

Broad Rights: *See* All Media.

Buyout: Rather than paying a copyright owner on a royalty basis for every copy sold or manufactured, some licensors prefer to pay a one-off fee instead. This is a buyout.

Copyright: A form of protection provided for by international laws which allows the holder to publish, sell, or otherwise profit from creative property (including musical works).

Cue Sheet: The form supplied to performing-rights organizations that lists all the music used in a film or TV show, along with ownership information. This enables the PRO to pay the relevant people without actually analyzing the film or TV show themselves.

Deal Memo: A brief letter of agreement which sets out the terms of an agreement. Once signed, the letter is binding upon all parties who must then further negotiate a "long form" agreement with the finer points included which will then supersede the deal memo. A deal memo is particularly beneficial when time is tight—such as clearing music for an upcoming TV show—as it allows parties to agree on the important contractual points in a short amount of time.

Deferred Payment: A one-off payment or series of timed payments that are dependent upon certain milestones being reached (such as a film being sold to a distributor, box office receipts, etc.)

Featured Use: Refers to the prominence of a piece of music in a film or TV show. If it is classed as "feature," it is usually the focus of the scene with little or no dialogue.

Indemnification: The protection, by you, of another party from any loss resulting from your contractual agreement

Licensing: The granting of rights to a named party, allowing them to legally use a piece of music.

Licensee: The third party who wishes to use music in their project.

Licensor: The owner of the copyright who grants permission to the licensee.

Long Form: The full and entire agreement between the licensee(s) and licensor(s).

Mechanical Rights: The right to reproduce a specific copyright in "mechanical" form. It is the property of whoever created the work, but is frequently assigned by them to a publisher. The publisher then grants mechanical licenses to companies who wish to, for example, reproduce the work on CD or DVD.

Needledrop: Sometimes music is licensed according to how many times the track is used rather than length or other measurement. This is known as "needledrop," or occasionally "laserdrop."

Option: An option gives the holder the right, at their own discretion, to make a specific agreement at a specific point in the future. For example, a Licensee may be granted the option to extend the terms of a licensing agreement for a set period of time before it is due to expire. This may be important to the licensee as he will want to ensure that he could use the specified piece of music for as long as he needs it but does not want to pay a large fee upfront for multiple years of usage.

PRO: Performing-rights organization, such as ASCAP, BMI, or PRS.

Short Form: *See* Deal Memo.

Show Reel: A compilation of work, intended to demonstrate the abilities of its creator. A musician's show reel would typically be on CD or perhaps video/DVD.

Sting: A short musical phrase, like a mini-jingle, and often a condensed version of the main theme.

Temp Track: Music temporarily edited into a film or TV show, so that the producer and director can see how the pictures and music would work together when the soundtrack is complete.

Underscore: The music played under dialogue and sound effects.

Work for Hire: Music specifically commissioned for a film or TV show which, under the provisions of the U.S. Copyright Act, becomes the property of the commissioner rather than the creator (who is usually paid a flat fee).

Performing-Rights Organizations
BMI
www.bmi.com
320 West 57th St.
New York, NY 10019-3790
Tel: (212) 586-2000

10 Music Square East
Nashville, TN 37203-4399
Tel: (615) 401-2000

8730 Sunset Blvd., 3rd fl. West
West Hollywood, CA 90069-2211
Tel: (310) 659-9109

ASCAP
American Society of Composers, Authors, and Publishers
www.ascap.com
One Lincoln Plaza
New York, NY 10023
Tel: (212) 621-6000

7920 W. Sunset Boulevard, 3rd floor
Los Angeles, CA 90046
Tel: (323) 883-1000

Two Music Square West
Nashville, TN 37203
Tel: (615) 742-5000

SESAC
www.sesac.com
55 Music Square East
Nashville, TN 37203
Tel: (615) 320-0055

152 West 57th St., 57th floor
New York, NY 10019
Tel: (212) 586-3450

501 Santa Monica Blvd., Suite 450
Santa Monica, CA 90401-2430
Tel: (310) 393-9671

PRS
Performing Right Society
www.prs.co.uk
Copyright House
29-33 Berners St.
London W1T 3AB
United Kingdom
Tel: 020 7580 5544

APRA
www.apra.com.au
6-12 Atchison St.
St Leonards NSW 2065
Australia
Tel: 02 9935 7900

JASRAC
Japanese Society for Rights of Authors, Composers, and Publishers
www.jasrac.or.jp
3-6-12 Uehara
Shibuya Tokyo 151-8540
Japan
Tel: 03-3481-2121

Licensing Organizations

Harry Fox Agency
www.harryfox.com
711 Third Ave.
New York, NY 10017
Tel: (212) 370-5330

AMRA (American Mechanical Rights Agency, Inc.)
www.amermechrights.com
150 S. Barrington Avenue, Suite 1
Los Angeles, CA 90049
Tel: (310) 440-8778

MCPS (Mechanical-Copyright Protection Society)
www.mcps.co.uk
Copyright House
29-33 Berners St.
London W1T 3AB
United Kingdom
Tel: 020 7580 5544

GEMA
www.gema.de
Bayreuther Str. 37
10787 Berlin
Germany
Tel: 030-21245-00

Suggested Reading List

Getting the Best Score for Your Film by David Bell (Silman-James Press)
Aimed at the independent community, this book lets you see things from the perspective of the filmmaker who wishes to commission music.

The Reel World by Jeff Rona (Miller Freeman Books)
Another book about commissioning music for film and TV, but this time aimed at the musician.

The Indie Guidebook to Music Supervision for Films by Sharal Churchill (Filmic Press)
Written by a music supervisor, this is a thorough, if somewhat technical, book which is essential reading for anyone who wants a good understanding of music licensing agreements.

Knowing The Score: Film Composers Talk About the Art, Craft, Blood, Sweat, and Tears of Writing for Cinema by David Morgan (HarperEntertainment)
A compendium of sixteen interviews with top Hollywood composers.

Music Supervision: The Complete Guide to Selecting Music for Movies, TV, Games, & New Media by Ramsay Adams, David Hnatiuk, and David Weiss (Schirmer Trade Books)
A book that educates you about the other side of the business: Music supervision and the people responsible for licensing your music.

Suggested Websites
The Music Broker Network
www.themusicbroker.net
A subscription service that pitches unsigned music to film/TV projects, as well as record companies and music publishers. Mention this book to receive a 10% discount on membership fees.

TAXI
www.taxi.com
Another subscription service that pitches unsigned music to film/TV, record companies, and music publishers.

CueSheet
www.cuesheet.net
An e-mail publication that lists specific music requirements from film and TV projects in Europe and North America.

The Hollywood Reporter
www.hollywoodreporter.com
The latest film and TV industry news in tinseltown.

INDEX